The Crop
a novel

Rebekah Tucker-Motley

a traditional publisher of quality books
by creative writers of all genres

www.parsonsporchbooks.com

The Crop
ISBN: Softcover 978-1-955581-62-2

The Crop

Chapter One

"Daydreaming again?"

Ru'ah blinked back into reality. Shielding her eyes from the glaring desert sun she looked up into the face of Yri. She had indeed been daydreaming. But it was so much more than a daydream, it seemed so real. The warmth of loving arms holding her, her world made right. This daydream, this longing for a different reality had consumed her more and more over the past few months. As she approached her coming of age, her dream of a loving childhood was all she could think about. This childhood she had not had and never would have.

"Still daydreaming?" came Yri's voice.

"I can't help it," said Ru'ah, "it's the only thing that keeps me going, the only thing that makes this rote life manageable."

"'This rote life' is something you should be grateful for, you know it could be so much worse," said Yri.

Yri had always looking out for her. Really, Yri was the closest thing Ru'ah had to a mother. She had never known a life without Yri. Yet as much as they loved each other, it was not the same. Yri was not her mother. For one, Yri had her own child, Gand, who Ru'ah had grown up with. The family did have a way of including Ru'ah, saying there were already mouths to feed, what was one more, but Ru'ah could tell she was still an outsider to them. Welcomed in, of course, but an outsider nonetheless.

"You'd better get your head out of the clouds, they are expecting much out of you as you come of age," Yri warned Ru'ah as the two gathered up the fabrics they had been mending.

"How much more can they expect from me, they already work me to the bone," replied Ru'ah.

The two women were enslaved workers of Iddo and Yawen, Chief Priests of Negev, the temple city. They were the link between the people of the desert and the Great Fire worshiped by the whole realm. Pilgrims were constantly flooding Negev to have an audience with Iddo and Yawen. It helped that Negev was positioned perfectly between the two kingdoms, Enst and Kal'i. Whenever either city faced any kind of disaster, threat, or inconvenience, floods of people would come for sacrifice, advice, and to just been in the presence of the Chief Priests. If Ru'ah was being honest, she wasn't all too convinced of their powers. For as long as she could remember, she had been their acolyte. She worked closely with every aspect of their rituals. From sunup to sundown, and sometimes even late into the night, she was by their side: preparing the elements, providing needed materials, cleaning and sorting, and everything in between.

Yri thought so highly of Ru'ah's position. Ru'ah thought it was easy for Yri to think so highly of her position since Yri was a fabric worker. She did not have the same obligations as Ru'ah, and she did not have the same limitations as Ru'ah. Although enslaved, Yri could come and go as she pleased. She was not constantly under the watchful eyes of the Chief Priests. Like everyone in her position, Yri longed for freedom, yet she had her own home, her own clothing, her own family. Ru'ah had nothing to call her own.

"Ah come now, you mustn't think so negatively. You may be worked to the bone, but you are given great honor. You are welcomed into the temple. Not many people, slave or slaver, can say that," Yri said.

It was true, even those who came on pilgrimage could not enter the temple proper. That right was reserved solely for the Chief Priests and, by necessary extension, the acolyte.

"I know," said Ru'ah, "I just don't feel right, like something is missing, like something isn't right about me being there."

"What couldn't be right? You were chosen," said Yri.

"Chosen before I could even walk or talk, chosen before I could even think for myself," said Ru'ah.

"So they saw something in you that you couldn't even see yourself, is that so bad?" said Yri.

"It's not bad, I just don't think it's right. I think I should be able to speak for myself," said Ru'ah.

"Ha! What would you even say?" challenged Yri.

"I don't know," said Ru'ah, hanging her head. How could she explain this to Yri? How could she explain this to anyone?

This was just the way things were. Iddo and Yawen were in charge, they were the Chief Priests. Everyone else had to do as they said. That was just the way it was. The Chief Priests had said that Yri was to be fabric workers, so she was a fabric worker. The Chief Priests said that Ru'ah was to be their acolyte, and so she was. That was her lot in life.

The two women continued to walk in silence. This was a rare day that Ru'ah had to spend however she wanted. All was well with the surrounding kingdoms, so the temple was not in use. Even Iddo and Yawen enjoyed these rare days of rest. They extended this rest of Ru'ah and she did not want to waste the day arguing with Yri.

As the two drew nearer to Yri's home, they could smell the fresh meal being prepared. This was one benefit of being enslaved to the Chief Priests - there was no shortage of food and water. Even when slaves were sent to travel throughout the desert, there was enough to pack to make it to the destination. And Yri's spouse, Beng, was a marvelous cook. He was always trying new ways of preparing food. Ru'ah really did count herself lucky to be invited into this home.

"Come, take a seat, the meal is almost ready!" Beng called out to Yri and Ru'ah as they came closer to the home.

"It smells wonderful as always," replied Yri, "and you are a sight for sore eyes."

"You are a sight to behold in my eyes," said Beng as he held his spouse close. The two embraced long enough for the children to take notice and beg to join in. Their own child, Gand, was a member of the scouts and was often away, but the house was always full from the children Beng was charged with caring for.

This was their nightly ritual. Yri would return from her long hours of work to a home filled to the brim with love. The two partners loved and supported one another through all times. This was the family Ru'ah never had, and the love she so longed for.

Her life was planned out before her. She was the acolyte. She would never unite with a partner or have her own family. She would serve the temple until the day she died.

Perhaps Ru'ah was wearing her thoughts on her face because just at that moment all seven of the young children came and surrounded her.

"Tell us news"

"What of the temple?"

"You have to share the latest!"

They called out as they embraced her. Ru'ah could not help but laugh. She knew they loved her company, but more than that, the children loved hearing her stories. She knew she could not share everything, but she loved the thrill of a good story as much as anyone else did.

"Tell us, tell us," they chanted.

"Now, now, I'm sure Ru'ah and Yri would like the warm meal I have prepared. Perhaps we could eat first and then share later," interrupted Beng.

Ru'ah was grateful for the distraction; it would give her time to decide which story to tell. She also wanted to have a little fun of her own. As they ate the delicious meal, she made sure to take her time. Every bite drawn out and savored. She had to close her eyes to keep from laughing at the exacerbated looks on the children's faces.

"Ok, ok. Are you ready?" Ru'ah asked the room.

"Yes!" Came the cheers.

"Here is what I have to say. Last week the Prince of Enst came for his annual blessing. All was going well from where I could see. The ritual has been prepared, the elements had been set, the prince was invited to his usual spot at the entrance of the temple. But that's when things started to go wrong. He insisted on entering. Iddo and Yawen had to physically block him from coming any closer. He shouted and demanded to know why he could not enter. I was amazed, no one had ever questioned such as thing before, not that I have ever known. He would not take no for an answer, but the Chief Priests would not move!" Ru'ah had to stop to catch her breath and take in the looks of amazement before her.

"Everyone knows that only the Chief Priests are allowed to enter, so why this prince thought he could, I cannot understand. But finally, he gave up. He turned to leave without the blessing. As he walked down the grand stairs, he suddenly stopped, turned and said, 'You'll regret this!' before leaving."

All around the room she saw the weight of her story take hold. No one ever threatened the Chief Priests. And yet this prince dared to not only question the tradition of the temple, but then to give this last threat was truly unbelievable.

That should satisfy the children's need for temple stories for a while.

The night wore on with more stories shared. Not temple stories, but the stories they all knew. Stories of valor and glory, stories of love. As far as Ru'ah was concerned, Beng was the best storyteller there was. Truly, as far as Ru'ah was concerned, Beng could do no wrong, she loved him so much. She knew her destiny was to the temple but she longed to be able to find a partner who loved her the way Beng loved Yri, and to love a partner the way Yri loved Beng.

After many hours of being surrounded by such love, it was time for Ru'ah to once again leave for her own quarters. She did not have her own home like Yri and Beng. Instead, she had a room inside the temple. That way she could be ready whenever the time came that

Iddo and Yawen needed her. She had a dreadful feeling that they would need her far too early in the morning.

As she said her final goodbyes to the children, promising to be back soon with more temple news, she felt the familiar hand of Yri on her shoulder.

“Let me walk you out, at least to the old tree,” Yri insisted. It was not unusual for Yri to walk Ru’ah to the massive tree that marked the center of the temple city, but something in Yri’s voice alarmed Ru’ah.

“Are you concerned?” asked Yri as they walked out the door.

“About what?” replied Ru’ah

“About the Prince, and his threat,” said Yri.

“Oh, I don’t think so. He was overstepping his bounds, but I doubt there is much to worry about,” said Ru’ah.

“Promise me you will do what you can to keep yourself safe,” said Yri.

This was such odd talk coming from Yri. They both knew the temple was the safest place in the city. Perhaps this was just maternal instinct kicking in.

“I promise,” said Ru’ah, hoping to satisfy Yri’s concern.

The two reached the old tree and embraced one last time for the night. Ru’ah breathed in the familiar scent of Yri and held on a little longer than usual. She may have not had the love of a mother in childhood, but Yri really was as close as she had. She should appreciate her more.

“Chin up,” said Yri before turning to head to her home for the night. Ru’ah made her way up the grand stairs, through the temple doors, and into her room. As she laid down her daydream returned. She drifted off to sleep knowing that her life was planned until the day she went to final rest.

Just as she had feared, she was awoken too early for her comfort the next morning. She did not consider herself lazy by any means, she just liked the idea of waking up after the sun.

Iddo and Yawen were benevolent masters to their enslaved workers, so Ru'ah tried not to show any dissatisfaction in front of them. Ru'ah had heard tale of masters who abused their slaves to the point of causing a riot. But not the priests. They ensured the safety, health, and well-being of all in the temple city. Nevertheless, an enslaved life was still an enslaved life. Ru'ah lived by the law of the land, and that was to obey Iddo and Yawen. So, when Iddo entered her room to announce it was time to rise, that is what Ru'ah did.

"To start the day, the usual chores are needed. I expect you to be back before the midday meal." Iddo told Ru'ah before abruptly leaving the room and entering the temple.

And so, another day began: Counting the wicks to insure there were enough for the monthly rituals, checking in with the scouts to see if there were any approaching pilgrims, gathering the elements needed for blessings. Bread and doves were the usual elements needed, but occasionally a ritual called for a strong wine as well. This was her life; this was her routine. It wasn't difficult labor; it was just what it was.

However, since Ru'ah could do these chores without much thought, it did free her mind to daydream. Once again, her mind went to her usual escape: being held in the arms of someone who truly loved her, feeling the warmth and peace of knowing that no matter what she would be protected and provided for. How lovely that would be.

There seemed to be sufficient wicks for the month, Ru'ah discovered. On to speak to the scouts. Since Ru'ah was the temple acolyte she was somewhat of a city celebrity. Everyone knew her, and she tried her best to know everyone as well. While the city was by no means large, Ru'ah simply did not have the time to socialize like others. Her rare days off were usually spent with Yri and Beng. Yet, she did make a point to greet everyone she met throughout the day.

"Coming to spy on us?" Gand inquired as Ru'ah approached the scout hut.

"Of course not!" Ru'ah replied, her cheeks turning red.

Gand laughed as he welcomed Ru'ah into the hut.

"No need to spy, I'll gladly tell you everything I know." Gand said while batting his eyes. He was the only child of Yri and Beng, had not yet found a partner to unite with. He was known around the city as a charmer. He would draw a suitor in with his smile, only to uncommit as soon as a new suitor caught his eye. Ru'ah and Gand had practically grown up together. At first, she had been captivated by him and thought perhaps he was true about his way with her, but she soon realized that was his way with everyone. She now laughed off his flirtation.

"Any news from the night watch?" Ru'ah went about her chore of inquiring of pilgrims.

"None," said Gand. "It's odd, the pilgrims who do come are coming from Kal'i in the south, but pilgrims from Enst in the North have all but stopped ever since the prince left in disgrace."

"Perhaps there is a block in the path," said Ru'ah.

"Perhaps," said Gand. "I will go out to scout as far as I can to see about a block. But the Wise Scout shows great concern."

The Wise Scout, the leader of the scouts, had been in that position for many years. She held the knowledge of the past and could compare it to the present. If she was concerned, perhaps Ru'ah should tell Iddo and Yawen.

"I appreciate your warning. I will inform the priests." Ru'ah said before turning to leave.

"One more week, correct?" asked Gand with a wink.

"Correct," said Ru'ah with a coy smile. While she did not take his flirting seriously, it did feel nice to be flirted with.

It would seem that the news of her coming of age had spread throughout the city. Maybe Yri is planning something big, thought Ru'ah.

In one week's, time she would indeed be of age. Ordinarily, that would mean she could become a suitor and look for a partner to unite with. But, she knew that was not the case for her.

She looked up at the sun – she had better hurry to the market for the elements in order to return to the temple before midday meal.

The market was crowded that morning, but due to her position as the acolyte, the crowds made way for her. All the enslaved folks of the city knew to give preference to the work of the temple.

"A pounding of bread?" asked Caff, the bread maker.

"Yes please," said Ru'ah.

She then turned around to call out for the package of doves needed from Niv, the dove keeper.

After gathering these elements, she headed back to the temple.

The sun beat down upon her as she finished her journey. It would soon be the hottest part of the year. As she climbed of the grand stairs, she thought once more of the warning from the scouts. She would indeed tell Iddo and Yawen of the Wise Scout's concerns, but she was sure there was really nothing to worry about.

"Just in time, have a seat," Yawen said as Ru'ah entered the meal room after putting away the elements.

Yawen was seated at one end of the table while Iddo was at the other. Ru'ah sat in between.

"Any news from the city?" Yawen asked.

Unlike Yri and Beng's children, Yawen was not looking for a good story. He wanted to know what was going on in the city so that he could keep a close watch on anything that seemed suspect.

"No news from the city," said Ru'ah. "But there is news from the scouts."

"Go on," said Yawen.

"The Wise Scout is concerned about the lack of pilgrims coming from Enst in the North, especially after the prince left. I told them to check for a blockage in the path, surely something is causing a delay," Ru'ah reported.

The atmosphere in the room changed. Yawen, who never showed his feelings, looked worried for only a split second.

Iddo looked from her spouse to Ru'ah and back to Yawen as if to read their thoughts before taking control of the conversation.

"Yes, a blockage, I'm sure," said Iddo. "The scouts will assess and report, no need for further discussion."

Ru'ah had never experienced anything like that before. Nothing ever rattled the priests; they were always in control. And yet, even for a moment they were scared? Surely not, surely Ru'ah was reading too much into what she thought she saw. Surely, it was the lack of sleep playing tricks on her.

"As you know, Ru'ah your coming of age will take place next week, therefore after the midday meal Yawen and I will be introducing you to a new ritual you will be assisting in," Iddo continued.

A new ritual. This piqued Ru'ah's curiosity. She had been serving as an acolyte from her childhood and thought she knew all the rituals by now. She was excited about anything that would be new and different.

They ate the rest of the meal in silence. This was quite different from the joyous meal at Yri and Beng's home. Iddo and Yawen were not joyous. They did not have time for idle chitchat. But there was an odd comfort eating in silence with the two priests. Ru'ah was glad she did not have to entertain them and was glad they only shared with her the necessary information. She much preferred eating with them than to eating completely alone, but she did not feel any familial comfort with them. Theirs was a working relationship and that was all. She preferred it that way and knew they did too.

With lunch eaten and the table cleared, it was time for the new ritual. Ru'ah could feel the excitement well up in her stomach. As usual the three entered the temple room called the Realm and anointed themselves with oil. This was the most crucial part of any ritual, since it set the tone.

This oil, according to the two priests, was holy. It was not bought in the market like the rest of the elements. Instead, Ru'ah pressed the oil from olives grown right behind the temple. Like the temple, no one was allowed in the olive grove except herself and the two priests. The priests used the oil to start each and every ritual.

First Iddo, then Yawen, and finally Ru'ah would submerge and thoroughly wash their hands in the oil. Then they would splash their face and hair with the same oil. Finally, they would take the oil that was dripping off their hair and wipe their feet clean.

Once Iddo, Yawen, and Ru'ah had completed the oil washing, they all entered the Realm. For every ritual, the priests would go to the center of the room where the altar was located while Ru'ah went to her corner, waiting for her turn to bring items needed. However, this time Iddo lead her to the center altar.

How odd, Ru'ah thought. She had never been so close to the altar before. She could see the intricate carvings that told stories from the past – the story of the Great Fire presenting itself to the people for the first time so long ago. The story of when the Great Fire destroyed a whole kingdom after the priest neglected to give proper homage. The story of the Great Fire splitting itself up to keep people warm during the legendary cold.

The Great Fire was their life, not just the Chief Priests, but everyone's. Without the Great Fire, none would survive. It was responsible for every blessing and every tragedy. The Great Fire gave, and the Great Fire took away. That was why it was so important to pay homage. Every ritual, every blessing, everything that happened in the temple was to pay homage to the Great Fire. The altar that Ru'ah was before was where the rituals took place.

She looked around at Iddo and Yawen trying to catch one of their eyes. Why was she here? But neither of them would make eye contact with her, their focus was on the altar.

She had grown accustomed to this. That is what they did for every ritual. She could tell what element they needed just by their stance and body language. She knew that when Yawen stretched his arm up he was in need of a dove. She knew when Iddo tilted her head to the right, she needed a piece of bread. She knew when the two united hands they needed wine. But she had the advantage of being in the corner, watching their movement. Here, right next to them, she would not sure how she should respond.

As if to answer her question Iddo took her by the hand, led her upon the altar, and gestured that she should lay down. Every fiber of her being was screaming that something was wrong. Why would she lay upon the sacred altar? She had never seen anyone do such a thing. And yet she followed what Iddo was leading her to do.

As she lay facing the ceiling she tried to daydream, she tried to feel the warmth of arms holding her, but the stone altar was so cold she would feel nothing. In her periphery, she could see the two priests circling her, yet she was unfamiliar with the gestures they formed. Tears silently fell from her eyes as she tried not to think about what was happening to her.

All at once, she felt a cold liquid falling on her. She could smell the familiar scent of freshly opened wine. She felt two sets of hands rubbing her body. She saw a flash of a knife in Yawen's hands as he moved to her head.

Before she could scream, she felt a pull at her scalp, a scraping near her ear. Somehow, the pain she had expected was not there. Iddo helped her sit up. She saw under where her head was what looked like a small furry creature. It dawned on her what happened. She reached up and felt that half of her hair had been lopped off.

The ritual, it seemed, was not yet done. Iddo and Yawen kneeled before her and offered her bread to eat. She could not even fathom what was going on. Why would the Chief Priests kneel before her, a mere acolyte, enslaved to them? At first, she refused the bread, thinking she misinterpreted the offering, but when Yawen placed the bread into her hand, she knew she must eat it.

It was the most delicious bread she had ever tasted. Caff was a master bread maker, and this was a masterpiece. It was slightly sweet and somehow still warn. This was a delicacy fit for the Great Fire. Somehow, she was given this blessing to eat.

Ru'ah hadn't realized her eyes where closed until after she had swallowed the last of the bread. She opened them to see Iddo and Yawen still kneeled before her. Should she say something? Of course not, since all rituals were done in complete silence. She had no choice but to remain seated until the priests gave her further instructions. Yet they did not move. She looked around the room to see two doves laying on the acolyte table.

Every instinct in her body told her to remain perfectly still, yet something compelled her to rise. Her legs walked her over to the doves while her mind screamed to go back to the altar. It was like she was possessed. She reached for the dead birds and took them back to the priests. As if on cue the two rose, took the doves from her, and laid them on the altar. Iddo sparked a wick with the flint and steel and lit both birds on fire. The three watched in silence as the fire consumed the doves.

After what felt like an eternity, Iddo broke eye contact with the fire and turned to Ru'ah. Yawen turned and looked at Iddo. Finally, there would be an explanation to what just occurred.

Iddo took Ru'ah by the hand and let her out of the Realm. The three walked out of the temple doors and into the dimming sunlight. Silence remained. Ru'ah was becoming frightened. Dare she break the silence with all of her questions?

Before she could make a decision, Yawen started the evening chant.

This was the chant that ended each day, letting the enslaved people know that their work was complete, and they could return to their homes. This was not the explanation that Ru'ah had hoped for. When the chant was over Iddo and Yawen returned into the temple and headed to their united chambers. Ru'ah was all alone once more.

She sat down at the top of the grand stairs not knowing what to do. Should she wait for Iddo and Yawen to return? Something told her they were not going to. She longed to run to Yri, to be held and comforted but she could not bring herself to leave the temple, especially with her hair half gone.

Most of the people in the city kept their hair long out of convenience, only cutting it when necessary. Occasionally someone would choose to keep their hair short, especially if it made their job easier. But no one had a half-shaved head. What would people think? She was already so well known around the city, this would make her stand out even more. If the priests knew how much she longed to blend in, to be just one of the crowd, would they have done this to her? Would they have even chosen her as an acolyte?

She doubted they cared much what she thought; they had never shown concern for her feelings before. She had never expressed her feelings to them. That just wasn't how it was done.

She looked out into Negev as the stragglers made their way home. The sun sank in the sky. She shivered with cold, but couldn't make herself move. If it were up to her, she would never return to the temple. But it was not up to her. Soon her weariness took hold. Forcing herself to open the temple door, she made her way to her room. This has been nothing like the day she thought it would be. This has been anything but routine. As much as she feared a rote life, she now feared more what else Iddo and Yawen had in store for her future.

The sun rose over the dunes, making its way to light the temple city. Ru'ah felt the warmth flowing in through her window as her eyes opened to greet the day. Today was the day. After 18 long years she was finally coming of age. As she lay on her mat, watching the rays of the sun dance with the shadows, she through about all she had been through to get to this point.

Her first memory was of the temple. She did not run and play in the grounds as most young children did. For her, playtime was in the quite moments after the rituals were completed and Iddo and Yawen went to their united chamber. Instead of making dolls and playing house, she would clean and organize the elements; often times speaking to them as if they were friends.

She thought about the first time she met Yri. She was in the market waiting for bread when this beautiful woman approached her. Yri spoke to Ru'ah as is she had known her for years. Of course, everyone knew her, she had been the little temple girl. She did not know Yri but felt an immediate kinship with the stranger. Yri helped Ru'ah with her morning chores that day and for many days afterwards. Looking back, it seemed that Yri was her guardian, someone meant to watch over her. She knew that wasn't the case – Iddo and Yawen were her only guardians. Yri was simply a friendly face.

Ru'ah thought about the one and only time she ever asked the priests about her parents. Even as a young child she knew the silence that met her questions meant it was not a topic for further discussion. She asked Yri later in life, but again was met with only silence. It must be that she was the only child in the city, or maybe even the world, that did not have parents at all.

She really should get up and start her chores, but the sun felt so good on her cold skin, and it was her coming of age day. Surely the priests would let her have the morning to herself.

It was not to be.

As soon as she had the thought, Iddo entered her room.

"It is time to rise, Ru'ah. Chores are waiting," came the cold voice.

"Yes, Iddo, I am getting up now," replied Ru'ah.

"I do know what day it is; do not think that I don't. There will be time to celebrate later," said Iddo.

This was a surprise. The two priests have not often acknowledged her aging day in past years, so Ru'ah had little expectation they would remember today. Yet, Iddo not only remembered, she said there would be a celebration. Had Yri invited the priests after all? Surely it was Yri's doing. Her friend had not discussed any plans with Ru'ah but she had been expecting a surprise celebration for the past few days since hints had been dropped here and there by members of the city as she did her daily chores. No one in the temple city had the ability to keep a secret.

But, no time to lose. As Iddo had said, there were chores to do. Ru'ah was no longer hoping to get out of them because they would provide the needed distraction from the excitement she could barely contain. And her fears about her hair seemed to be unnecessary, as no one in the city had yet to mention it.

Making her way through the market, Ru'ah made a point to walk by Yri's workspace. She saw her friend hunched over a tattered piece of fabric and hesitated to interrupt. Yri took her work very seriously. She was always kind, but Ru'ah could tell she got frustrated when her concentration was broken. She began to leave but turned around again when she heard the unmistakable sound of Yri saying hello.

"I am sorry if I distracted you," Ru'ah apologized.

"No need, I know you were about to leave but I couldn't let you go without an age day hug. Plus, I was at a good stopping point anyway," Yri laughed as she embraced Ru'ah.

"You remembered!" Ru'ah said with a grin.

"Remembered? How could I forget! This is only one of the most important days of your life. You are of age!" replied Yri.

Ru'ah's grin grew even wider. "I am so excited for the celebration tonight, don't pretend to not know what I speak of. The whole city has been abuzz."

"The city might be abuzz but it is certainly not my doing," said Yri.

"Ah, right, well then I best get back to my chores and let you do the same," replied Ru'ah, still grinning. She knew Yri had indeed been involved in the city buzz, whether or not she would admit it.

"Yes, chores must be done in order to enjoy a nice evening," said Yri with a wink.

With that, the two friends separated, looking forward to whatever the evening would bring.

Time dragged on the rest of the day as Ru'ah completed her chores. Foot traffic in the temple was still slow so she only had to help with one ritual that afternoon.

It seemed as if the day would never end, but sure enough right on time, Yawen chanted and the workday was over. Ru'ah swelled with excitement. It was time for the celebration. It was only then that she realized she didn't actually know when or where the celebration was going to be.

She had expected some sort of invitation to arrive, or maybe even Yri herself to inform her of what was going on, but throughout the day no such information presented itself. She had no choice but to do what she always did at the end of a workday. She returned to her room hoping that maybe a clue would be waiting for her.

To her surprise, there was nothing out of the ordinary in her room. Since Yri was not allowed in the temple Ru'ah knew not to expect her to show up. This was odd. Perhaps she had miss-interpreted what was happening in the city. Had she imagined all the hints she was sure she heard?

The sun sank low in the sky right along with her heart. Iddo said there would be a celebration, maybe Ru'ah should try to find her.

As she approached the united chamber of Iddo and Yawen her could hear her heartbeat grow louder and louder. Only in the most dire of circumstances was she supposed to enter their chamber. This was certainly not a dire circumstance. But, how else would she find out about the celebration?

Just as she gathered up the courage to knock, the familiar cold voice sounded behind her.

"Ru'ah, follow me," said Iddo.

Relieved, Ru'ah turned from the door and did what she was told.

"I am sorry Iddo, I was only going to ask you about the celebration you spoke about this morning," Ru'ah said. But her explanation was met with silence. Iddo led Ru'ah to the main door, where Yawen was waiting for them.

"For 18 years you have been our faithful acolyte, and now it is your coming of age day," said Yawen.

This was quite unexpected. Yawen rarely showed any emotion, but Ru'ah thought she heard the slightest catch in his throat.

Yawen continued, "Today we mark your official entrance into your next stage in life. While you will remain an acolyte your duties will increase, as will your standing."

With that, the two priests grabbed Ru'ah hands. She felt a light squeeze from both before they released her from their grip.

The two priests moved towards the doors and pushed them open, revealing before Ru'ah's eyes the entire city standing right in front of the temple.

She barely had time to understand what was happening before the music started up and she was led down the grand stairs.

This was her coming of age celebration. It was not indeed planned by her friend Yri, but by her masters, the two people she least expected to join in her celebration. Perhaps she had misjudged their coldness towards her. Could they in fact care about her?

Before she could think too long about that, Yri and Beng engulfed her in a hug.

"It was so hard to keep this from you, especially this morning!" Yri shouted above the music.

"How long have you known?" asked Ru'ah

"Months and months. Iddo and Yawen wanted this to be a celebration to remember!" replies Yri.

Ru'ah had so many more questions that she could not ask because at that moment four of the children Beng took care of rushed toward her.

"Happy coming of age day!" They shouted.

"Everyone is here, meals have been prepared, and there is music and dancing. I've never seen a celebration like this," said Beng. "What would you like to do first?"

How could Ru'ah make that decision, she was overwhelmed. Thankfully, her stomach answered for her.

"I think it is time for the evening meal, don't you?" Ru'ah posed to the group.

"Let us go find a good feast!" said Beng and led the way to the booths.

Truly everyone was there. Ru'ah greeted Caff who offered her several loaves of bread to share with Yri, Beng and the children. Niv has prepared doves in various sauces and spices. Delicacies and sweet treats lined the surrounding booths all ripe for the choosing.

With full bellies and full hearts, Ru'ah and the rest decided to make their way to the dancing. Ru'ah was not much of a dancer, but loved seeing the twirling and swirling moves, especially when the united couples would dance as if they were one.

Beng and Yri took hold of one another to enter into a dance as soon as they arrived. Ru'ah was happy to stay with the children. Although one by one they each entered the dance as well. She sighed in deep contentment as she watched these partners that she loved enjoy themselves so much at her celebration.

She would have been fine watching the dance all night, but someone else had other plans. Out from the crowds appeared Gand to ask her to join in with him.

As much as she knew he was a charmer, she could not resist that smile, not tonight anyway. The two spun around and around to the music, first fast, then slow then fast again. As another slow dance started Ru'ah found herself reeling from thoughts about what life could be. She did not want to be partners with Gand, but feeling him hold her made her yearn for that life once more. She tried to shoo away those thoughts and just enjoy the night, but they were persistent.

"I must leave you now, Gand," Ru'ah said above the noise.

"Ah, well I thank you for the time spent with me," Gand said with a wink. Before Ru'ah was even out of area, Gand had embraced Caff in another dance.

Yri, Beng and the children had also disappeared into the crowd. Ru'ah was once again alone. This was a feeling she had become used to over the many years and a feeling she would live with for the rest of her life. She wanted so much to enjoy the rest of the evening, but this thought made her want to retire.

No one will even notice if I am gone, Ru'ah thought. The celebration was in full swing, with no sign of letting up. She decided to make her way back to her small room in the grand temple.

She made it all the way to the grand stairs before she was spotted.

"Retiring so soon?" came the cold voice of Iddo.

"I thank you for this wonderful celebration," said Ru'ah. "I just fear I am too tired to continue with it."

"Before you go, would you spend a few moments with us?" Asked Iddo as she gestured to where she and Yawen had been sitting.

Had they been there this whole time? Thought Ru'ah. It was true they tried to keep themselves separate from their enslaved workers, but they had gone through all this trouble to plan this celebration. Surely they should be out enjoying it.

Ru'ah took a seat in between the two priests. The wind started to pick up. The half of her head that had been shaved tingled with the cold. Her long hair on the other side whipped into her face. She waited and waited for either of the priests to say anything. But the three of them set in complete silence.

It was as if they were at their evening meal. No one spoke, but there was a familiar comfort nonetheless. Ru'ah started to sense that Yawen and Iddo were enjoying themselves as they watched their enslaved workers enjoy themselves. Ru'ah knew them to be benevolent, but she was still surprised at this reaction. No one ever spoke ill of the two priests, not that she had heard anyway. They did their best to provide for the whole city. Yet she had assumed it was out of obligation, so that the enslaved workers would not riot. Could it be genuine affection instead of obligation? She had been surprised by this celebration, perhaps she had more to learn about these two priests than she knew. Perhaps they too longed for freedom for their workers.

After what seemed like hours of sitting in silence, Iddo finally broke in. "This night has been for you. Tomorrow the work begins."

Yawen started to chant the end of workday chant.

As if by some spell, the music and dancing stopped. Workers returned to their booths to clean and pack up. Would they have to be ready at first light in the morning? Thought Ru'ah. Hopefully this celebration did not interfere with the next day's work.

Ru'ah watched as all the people gathered their families and headed back to their homes. This night would be the talk of the city for quite some time. She truly hoped everyone enjoyed it.

Soon Yawen and Iddo rose to walk up the grand stairs. She knew she should follow but couldn't make herself get up yet. As tired as she had been she was now rushing with adrenaline. It was as if Iddo's words had finally sunk in.

The real work begins tomorrow? What could that possibly mean?

Chapter Two

Whatever Iddo had intended by those words did not become immediately clear. The next day started out business as usual. Ru'ah was awoken right as the sun rose in the sky.

She made her way to the morning meal, to find Iddo and Yawen halfway through eating. They did not usually wait for her, but she thought after last night they would be more willing to include her. But even as she tried to make small talk they would not engage. It seemed to Ru'ah that things had not changed after all, life in the temple was as it had always been.

After the morning meal, Iddo approached Ru'ah, but only to reminder to get more wine while she went about her chores. Ru'ah shook off her initial disappointment. She was quite interested to see how the city was fairing after the celebration of the night before.

To her surprise, it really was business as usual in the city. Not a soul looked even remotely tired. Not even Gand, who she was sure stayed up well past Yawen's chant.

"Well if it isn't my favorite dance partner," Gand called out as soon as he saw her coming toward the scout hut.

"Good morning to you. I trust you took full advantage of the fun last night," replied Ru'ah.

"How could I have had fun when you disappeared so soon into the night," said Gand.

Something was different about the way Gand looked at her this morning. Perhaps he had finally noticed that half her hair was missing. But his look was not one of disgust, more intrigue, as if he was seeing her for the first time. The look he gave her was the one she imagined was the one united partners gave to one another. Ru'ah reminded herself that Gand was still the city charmer, and to not take any look he gave her too seriously.

"I am sorry for disappearing, I was just becoming overwhelmed by the festivities," Ru'ah said.

"Overwhelmed? The festivities were in your honor, it was your night to shine," teased Gand. Ru'ah knew that if the celebration had been for Gand it would have never ended. He was the type who would dance all night and not feel a thing the next day. She, on the other hand, become tired just by walking through the market. Perhaps it was because Gand was already used to being around people so much, and she of course was not. She laughed off his teasing.

"Well, today I must ask about the route to the North, has the blockage been found yet?" Ru'ah changed the subject, getting down to business.

The smile vanished from Gand's lips. "We have been sending scouts out further and further each day. There was a set who were sent out on an overnight mission – you know how much the Wise Scout hesitates to send scouts out overnight – well, I am afraid to say, it was as I said, no blockage has been found," Gand said.

This was quite a surprise for Ru'ah, as she was sure there would be a blockage. This morning had not gone the way she had expected at all.

"What does the Wise Scout say now?" Ru'ah asked,

"I think it best you speak to her directly," said Gand. "I will take you now."

Ru'ah hesitated. Should she spend more time with the scouts? She still had to go to the market and return to the temple before midday meal. If she fell behind with these morning chores, she would not be available to help with the afternoon rituals. She feared to keep Iddo and Yawen waiting. But she also did not want to ignore the Wise Scout. Perhaps she would need to deliver this news to the priests.

After a moment, she decided to chance missing midday meal to speak to the Wise Scout. Gand led the way into the hut where she could be found.

"Greetings Wise Scout," Ru'ah said as she approached Tell.

"Greetings Ru'ah, it has been some time since we last spoke, but I would like to say congratulations on your coming of age. I did enjoy the celebration last night," Tell said.

Ru'ah would never admit it, but she was envious of Tell. Not only was Tell the Wise Scout of the scouts and therefore well respected, she was also very beautiful. Ru'ah couldn't help but notice how her hair flowed in the slight breeze and her eyes glistened in the sun.

Ru'ah could only reply with a grin.

"But now I must give you the news I have feared to say," Tell began again, this time with a tone that let Ru'ah know to take this seriously.

"As I'm sure Gand has told you there is no blockage in the route to Enst in the North. However, news has come to us that the prince is refusing to allow his citizens to come to the temple city until Iddo and Yawen allow him to see the Great Fire."

Ru'ah was taken aback. No one, not even the acolyte was allowed to see the Great Fire. That right was reserved only for the Chief Priests. Fear raced through her body at the thought of that changing.

"That simply cannot be done," Ru'ah finally replied.

"Of course not. The temple city will not be held hostage by a rouge prince," said Tell, with a fierceness only the Wise Scout could possess.

"I will tell the priests of this news," said Ru'ah softly. She did not want to invoke that fierce tone from Tell again.

"And we will continue to scout out the route to Enst to see if we can gather more news," said Tell.

Gand led Ru'ah out of the hut into the fresh air. This morning was not going as planned at all, thought Ru'ah.

"No one can see the Great Fire," Ru'ah said to herself.

"Not to worry, sweet Ru'ah, the scouts will take care of this rouge prince," said Gand.

Ru'ah looked up at Gand. Sweet Ru'ah? This was a new level of flirting. Even if she was allowed to unite with another, Gand would certainly not be her choice. What were his intentions?

Without saying anything else Ru'ah turned to go to the market. If she thought she had been overwhelmed by the celebration last night, that was nothing compared to how she felt already this morning.

But, there were still chores to be done. Ru'ah got the usual bread and doves from the market without much ado. Although she was surprised to see that how late the celebration went night seemed to not affect the market. Everyone was their usual friendly selves. She noticed more and more folks smiling at her than ever before. It was almost as if they were trying to get her to notice them. Did this happen to everyone when they came of age? Or maybe they were thankful for the celebration in her honor? As far as she knew nothing like that had ever happened before. Perhaps there was just a collective excitement in the air.

"Good morning Soph," Ru'ah called out to get Soph, the master wine maker's, attention. She was friendly but mostly no-nonsense. Hers was usually the busiest booth, so she had to keep conversations light and quick. This morning Ru'ah was glad for that since she did not have much energy for conversation.

"The usual?" Soph called back.

"Yes, please," said Ru'ah.

With that, she was free to return to the temple.

The wine added extra weight so her moving was slower than usual. This did not work in her favor, as more and more city folk came up to her to say how much fun the celebration was last night. It wasn't that she did not want their company, it was just that she was already so overwhelmed. She felt herself becoming more and more curt with her responses. She was just about to reach her breaking point, when Beng and the children appeared.

"It looks like you might need some help," said Beng as he took the wine from her.

She had never been more thankful for his helping hand. Just his presence gave her a sense of ease. She wished she could explain how much she loved him. It wasn't the same way Yri loved him, she knew that. It was more of a comfort love, as if he was her protector. At that moment, she loved him so much she wanted to cry.

It must have shown of her face because Beng told the children to take the rest of her load and together they walked to the temple in silence.

How was it that Beng knew exactly what she needed? Just like Yri, Ru'ah felt that sometimes Beng could read her mind.

As the family approached the stairs, she gladly took her load back from them. Without a word, Beng hugged her. This was too much for her. She broke down in tears.

After a moment Beng simply said, "Chin up."

These words were all that Ru'ah needed to hear. She took a deep breath, gave Beng and all the children one last hug and began her accent of the grand stairs. She would forever be grateful for Beng and Yri. As much as she longed for a family of her own, they certainly made a wonderful substitute.

Ru'ah rushed to get the elements from the market put away and still barely made it on time to the midday meal. Iddo's eyebrow cocked as Ru'ah sat down as if in warning. Punctuality was of upmost importance in the temple. If the midday meal ran late, the afternoon rituals could not start on time.

As usual the meal was eaten in silence. Ru'ah tried to ease her mind after the hectic morning. She had almost calmed down when Yawen broke into her thoughts.

"News from the city?" he asked.

"None that I heard," she replied.

She needed to regather her strength before she shared with them the news from the scouts. After taking a breath, she continued. "However, I did speak with the Wise Scout."

At this, Iddo and Yawen stopped mid bite. They knew that if the Wise Scout spoke to the acolyte, it was dire news indeed.

When Ru'ah told them of Tell's message the air left the room. Iddo and Yawen sat in silence for a few more moments.

Ru'ah knew that the priests never rushed anything, yet their body language told her they were both concerned. Ru'ah herself was anxious about this news and was sure the priests were in shock. No one saw the Great Fire; how could the prince ever suggest that. Beyond that, she had no idea what they were thinking.

"That is certainly unexpected," Iddo finally said. "I will have to go to speak with the Wise Scout myself."

"Yes, that is probably for the best," agreed Yawen. "This is most unexpected."

With that, Iddo rose from the table. Once again, Ru'ah was surprised. She had never known a time when Yawen and Iddo were not together. Inside or outside the temple the two did everything as one. Perhaps this was meant as a tactic. If both Priests went to speak with the Wise Scout, surely that would cause a panic within the city. She tried to put it out of her mind as there were other chores needing her attention before the afternoon rituals could begin.

As she cleaned up the table it occurred to her that the scouts did not mention any pilgrims arriving today. Usually when that happened Yawen and Iddo gave her the day off, but they had not yet. Perhaps they would give her the afternoon. She was looking forward to spending more time with Yri. She had many questions about Gand and wanted to pick Yri's mind. As his mother, surely she had some idea of what he was thinking. She herself was completely thrown off by his actions this morning.

Ru'ah also wanted more time to calm down from feeling so hectic and anxious. She was not used to so much excitement in such as short amount of time. She longed for her quiet room to rest in the afternoon sun. She moved a little more quickly so that her chores would be done in no time.

After one final sweep of the meal room, Ru'ah stretched and decided to head to her room for a little while.

As she was leaving, she heard the faintest cough. Turning around she saw that Yawen had re-entered the meal room.

Ru'ah was genuinely surprised to see him as she had assumed he had gone back to his priestly duties.

And since Iddo had gone to talk to the Wise Scout Ru'ah found that she was alone in the meal room with Yawen. This had never happened before. She was not sure how to feel or how to act.

"Ru'ah I ask that you sit back in your chair," said Yawen softly.

Ru'ah had no choice but to obey. If one of the Chief Priests gave her an order that is what she would do.

Yawen said nothing else for such a long time that Ru'ah thought he might have fallen asleep. Perhaps he simply wanted company when Iddo was away.

Soon enough he spoke once again. "We are priests of the Great Fire, and you are our acolyte," he said.

Ru'ah was confused as to where this was going.

"The Great Fire was and is and shall be," Yawen continued. "At the beginning of all time the Great Fire conceived the desert. The heat we feel is but a glimpse of its burning heat. Long, long ago, out of the earth our ancestors came. One by one, they walked through the desert. They felt the heat, they learned how to survive."

Ru'ah had never heard this before. Was this another new ritual she must learn now that she was of age?

"For years and years our ancestors struggled. They fought with the Great Fire. They burned. Until one day a united couple had an idea, an idea that came from the Great Fire itself. This idea was to not fight the Great Fire but submit to it. They gathered all sorts of materials: wood, cloth, food. They heaped these materials into a mound in the middle of the desert. They brought the Great Fire to the mound and there the Great Fire stopped. No longer did it burn cities or peoples. As long as the mound was fed with materials, it stayed.

For years the mound burned with the Great Fire. For years the people learned from the Great Fire. They were able to rebuild cities and bring portions of the Great Fire into their homes. During the cold times the Great Fire kept them alive with warmth. They learned that the Great Fire would bless their food. When they kept meat near the Great Fire it would become delicious to eat.

The united couple became the first Chief Priests all those years ago. But, as all humans do, they became older. They realized they could no longer maintain the mound. So, with the Great Fire's blessing, they took a portion of it into the temple. And from that day until this day that portion of the Great Fire continues to burn."

Ru'ah was enraptured by this story. She could not believe that she was hearing these things. Even more surprising was when Yawen stopped speaking and stood up.

"And now, you must come with me," he said.

Again, Ru'ah did as she was told, but this time it was with eagerness. She wanted to know the rest of Yawen's story. She followed him through the Realm and into the part of the temple she had never been to before. It was a small door located just beyond Iddo and Yawen's united chambers. The air grew colder and colder as they approached the door.

Yawen knelt down before the door and Ru'ah followed suit. Yawen chanted a prayer Ru'ah had never heard before.

The priests arose, and Ru'ah followed. He slowly opened the door. But before he entered, he turned to face Ru'ah.

He said so quietly that she had to strain to hear, "We are priests of the Great Fire, and you are our acolyte."

Finally, he entered the door and Ru'ah followed. There before her eyes was a wick burning with the brightest fire she had ever seen. She was compelled to fall down before it in reverence. This was the remnants of the Great Fire from all those years ago. This was the reason that Iddo and Yawen were Chief Priests, this was the reason she was their acolyte. This was the reason for not only their lives but for the lives of everyone in the desert. This was the Great Fire that was and is and shall be. And she, lowly enslaved acolyte that she was, had been blessed with this gift to come before it.

For the second time that day she broke into tears. Deep sobs welled up inside her and fell from her eyes. She did not deserve this, she did not deserve any of this. She did not deserve the family she found in Yri, Beng, and Gand. She did not deserve the way Gand had looked at her this morning. She did not deserve the celebration Iddo and Yawen and given her last night and she certainly did not deserve to come before the Great Fire. Who was she? No one. And so she sobbed. Her eyes ran out the pain and confusion she felt. Her eyes ran out the longing for a family of her own. Her eyes ran out her doubt of the rituals she helped perform. She cried and cried until all her strength was gone.

Yawen must have expected this kind of response because he let her cry for as long as she could. Ru'ah knew he was still there since she could feel his presence, but he did not interrupt or try to comfort. For what felt like an eternity the two of them remained before the fire, both in awe in their own ways. Finally, Ru'ah could cry no more.

She wiped away the last of her tears and rose to her feet. "I do not know why you showed this to me, but I thank you with all of my heart," she said to Yawen.

Yawen closed the door and knelt to chant another prayer. He then led Ru'ah back to the realm. The new ritual was not yet complete.

Once again Ru'ah was led in front of the altar. Having just heard the whole story of the Great Fire and seeing it for herself, she had new insight into the carvings on the altar. She had a newer, deeper appreciation of what the Great Fire meant. She was prouder to be so close to its altar. She thought that perhaps if Yawen and Iddo had shown her the fire before, she would have been a better acolyte, taking her responsibilities far more seriously.

Iddo and Yawen, the Chief Priests, the ones who taught her everything she knew, the ones who knew the whole story of the Great Fire. The ones who took the time and effort to plan a surprise coming of age celebration just for her. Perhaps she took them for granted. Perhaps she did not appreciate them the way she should.

She turned to look them in the eyes before the new ritual started but realized once again that Iddo was not there. She was totally alone with Yawen. She looked over at Yawen and what she saw frightened her.

His eyes shown like fire. They had a hunger she had never seen before, as if he had been waiting for this moment for a long time.

As exhausted as she was from the events of the day so far, every muscle in her body tensed up. She wanted so badly to run.

Yet she did not, she was trained well. Whatever the Chief Priests told her to do, she would do. Without mistake, Yawen told her to lay down on the altar. Just like the time before she felt the cold stone beneath her. Just like the time before she tried to shut her mind to what was going on around her. She tried to shut her mind to the fright she felt of being alone with Yawen. Where was Iddo? Still talking with the Wise Scout? Surely this ritual could wait for her return. But Yawen did not wait, he proceeded with that he had started.

She felt the familiar liquid poured all over her body. By its smell she could tell it was the new wine she had just purchased from the market. Was this a new ritual after all? Was this not the same as the time before? She hoped that it would be over just as quickly.

Ru'ah felt Yawen's hands all over her body. He kneaded her shoulders, her arms, her hands. He touched each finger, rubbing the wine into her skin. She felt him move to her legs and toes. She had nothing left to cry or else her tears would have mixed with the wine. She could not stand any more emotions this day. She had had enough.

She could think of nothing else to do but imagine the fire glowing in the room beyond her. She imagined its warmth on her skin instead of Yawen's hands. She imagined what it would have been like to be the first to be honored with the Great Fire. What was it like to have been the united couple who had learned how to tame it?

She imagined what it was like to eat that first food warmed by the fire. She thought of the meal she shared with Yri and Beng the night before. Perhaps that meal was a taste of what the Great Fire could do to meat. She thought of Gand and longed for him to be here with her. She did not know how she felt about him, but she knew he would protect her against any harm.

Her thoughts were once again interrupted by Yawen. He had finished with the wine. Just like the time before he brought out a knife and proceeded to her hair. She felt the same tug as he shaved off what was left of it. At least now she would not have to worry about standing out.

Yawen helped her sit up. She could not look at him but knew from the time before that he was kneeling before her with bread in his hands. She did not want to eat it. She did not want to have anything to do with this ritual anymore. But once again, as if her body was not her own, her hand reached out for the bread and led it to her mouth. The sweet bread filled her senses. It was indeed delicious. For one moment she did forget where she was and focused only on the bread.

As she finished the last piece, she opened her eyes to see that there was only one dove waiting for her. She did not wait for her legs to move her but went straight to retrieve the bird. She watched as Yawen took the wick and lit the dove on the alter.

When the bird was fully burned Yawen turned towards Ru'ah but just as the time before he did not say a word. He went straight out of the realm to start the end of day chant.

Ru'ah could not move. She could not bring herself to rise from where Yawen had left her. She felt a burning in her chest. At first it was a small flame, but slowly grew to fill her whole body. What was this new feeling inside her? She somehow felt older, stronger, wiser. Yet the same Ru'ah remained. She looked around the room and remembered all her times helping with different rituals. She thought of the times she brought elements to the priests. She thought of the times brining news to Yawen of the goings on of the city. She thought of all the pilgrims she had met over the years. Everything looked the same as it had for years. Everything felt and smelled the same as she had always known. Yet somehow, she knew the ritual she just went through would change everything. What her future held she was not sure, but she knew it would be different. She felt scared still, but she also felt like she could protect herself now, as if she had already gone through the worst.

Perhaps that was the point of this ritual after all. She now knew the truth of the Great Fire. She now had been through this ritual. Even though she still had so many questions she knew in time she would be wise to their answers.

Finally, she got herself off the floor. She stretched herself to her full height and walked a little taller. It was time for the evening meal, but she found she was not hungry. She made her way to her room, and fell into a deep, peaceful sleep.

The next thing Ru'ah knew she was surrounded by a strange crop. She looked around and could see nothing but this crop for miles and miles. She turned around and around until she finally saw a path. She did not know where she was, how she got there, or even what kind of crop this was that she was in. Yet she walked towards the path, hoping for a clue. She followed the path for what seemed like hours. On and on it went, winding around, never ending.

Until all of the sudden, it did. She had reached the end of the path, but instead of the temple city, she found she was in the middle of the desert. She started to become truly afraid. Where was she? How would she get home?

Ru'ah was on the verge of panic when she heard a voice. "You have made it," the voice said.

What a voice it was. It was the most beautiful sound Ru'ah had ever heard, and it immediately calmed her.

She turned around to see where the voice was coming from. At first, she could see no one, but a figure started to come out of the crop maze.

"You have made it," the voice repeated itself, "but now you must come back."

The figure with the most amazing voice beckoned her to come back into the crop maze. All of her doubts and fears about where she was vanished as she followed.

They walked on and on back into the crop maze without speaking. The figure was just a little ahead of her, just out of her reach.

It occurred to Ru'ah that she could in fact speak, so she asked, "Who are you?"

"I am the one you most want me to be," said the voice.

Ru'ah heart swelled. Could it be? Could this figure, the one who was leading her, be her mother?

Ru'ah was stunned back into silence. All she could do was keep walking, hoping to catch up. To her frustration, though, no matter how fast she would walk, the figure moved just a little faster. Ru'ah had broken into a run, but that still was not fast enough.

She had to keep trying. After years of longing and hoping for this moment, after the emotion and trauma of the past day and a half, after years of being alone, she could not let her mother escape her.

When she could not keep up the pace, she yelled out, "please stop, I need you!"

The figure stopped but did not turn around. "You do not have to run to me, I am right here, always," said the voice.

To Ru'ah's relief she was able to move closer to the figure without her moving away again. She reached out her hand to feel, for the first time, her mother. But her hand landed on nothing. She tried again and again her hand went straight through the figure.

"Child, be patient," said the voice.

Patient? Had she not been patient? How much longer would she have to wait?

The figure gestured towards the sky. Ru'ah looked up to see the starts shining. She had not realized it was still nighttime.

"Can you count them?" the voice asked.

Confused, Ru'ah concentrated on counting the starts, but soon found that she could not keep track of them.

Defeated, she shook her head.

"I can," said the figure.

Again, silence fell. Ru'ah wanted to say something but could not. No words seemed to be the right ones for this moment.

A slight breeze rustled the crops around her and Ru'ah inhaled deeply. The smell reminded her of how the bread tasted on the altar. Sweet and pure. Was this the wheat Caff used when making the temple bread?

"I made this for you," the voice said.

Ru'ah opened her eyes. "You made what for me?" she asked. But the voice did not respond. She went to move closer to the figure hoping to learn more, but the figure started to move away.

"I am always here," the figure said once more. But then in a flash it was gone. Ru'ah was once again completely alone in the middle of a crop maze.

She could not stop herself from shouting out, "Come back! Come back!" But she saw the figure no more and heard the voice no more.

After some time waiting, Ru'ah decided to head back out of the maze. She walked and walked, but never came to the desert she was in before. Could she be lost? She thought this was a straight path out, but maybe it really was a maze after all. She started to call out for the voice again when she felt a change in the air.

The sweet smell of the crop mixed in with another smell, a smell that filled her with fear.

The maze was on fire and she was in the middle of it.

Panic-stricken she started to run. Faster and faster she went until she could run no more. She looked up to realize she was completely surrounded by flames. Where was she? How did she get here? She wanted to go home.

"Help, help," she cried out.

"Mother come back!" tears poured down as the flames drew near. With her last breath, she let out one last scream for help.

Ru'ah awoke to find herself in her room in the temple. She was drenched in sweat. It had been a dream. It felt so real, but it had indeed been a dream.

Ru'ah had to reorient herself. Was she really back in her room? She could still feel the heat from the fire on her skin. She took a moment to catch her breath, but then remembered.

"Mother!" she cried out.

She had been so close to her mother, closer than ever before but still not close enough. What a cruel trick. Why wouldn't her mother let her get closer? For years she had longed to be held in her mother's arms, didn't her mother know that?

Ru'ah tried to cry but found that no tears would come. How much more of this could she take? She had never been so drained in her life. She lay back down, longing for sleep, longing for the dream to return. She would even take the fire if it meant seeing her mother again.

But nothing she did worked. She tossed and turned but could not get comfortable. She felt every crack in the floor beneath her sleeping pad. She finally decided to get up.

Ru'ah stood next to the window for some time, looking out at the city. It was so quiet and not a soul to be seen in the streets. All the families were tucked in their homes for the night. From her window, she could just barely see Yri and Beng's home. Her thoughts wondered. What was it like to have a family meal every night? What was it like to feel the security and love of a mother and father? She was so close to feeling that tonight, so close.

Her thoughts moved on to Gand. Since he was of age, he had his own home away from Yri and Beng but could still visit them as he pleased. They were still his family. What was he doing this night? Was he thinking of her? She thought back to that morning when he looked at her in that way. Will he look at me like that again tomorrow? She thought.

She looked up at the stars and remembered what the voice asked her. She once again tried to count them but once again lost track. Who could count the stars? Her mother could.

Her mother! Would she ever see her again? She was out there somewhere. At least in her dreams. But it couldn't have been just a dream, it felt too real. Maybe her mother was sending her a message. That would mean her mother really was out there, somewhere.

"Mother, come back!" Ru'ah cried out into the wind.

It was no use, her mother was gone again. The stars shown down, the city nestled into the night. Ru'ah thought about laying back down, but knew she would not be able to get back to sleep.

Feeling parched, she decided to go to the meal room for some water. Perhaps where would even be some evening meal left over.

She quietly opened her door and tiptoed to the meal room, hoping not to disturb Iddo and Yawen. But to her surprise, as she got closer to the meal room, she heard the familiar voices of the two priests.

She had not disturbed them. They were up already and in a heated discussion.

Ru'ah knew she should not listen in but couldn't resist. She had never heard either Iddo or Yawen raise their voice. What could have upset them so?

"I don't care what the Wise Scout says, I will not allow it," Yawen seethed.

Ru'ah remembered that Iddo had gone to speak with the Wise Scout that day. She knew what Tell would say but didn't think it would upset Yawen this much. Perhaps there was more to the story than she knew.

"Yawen, it might be worth at least considering," replied Iddo, "A bend might be necessary in order for the tradition to stand."

"Tradition! You speak of tradition! You do not understand the tradition like I do," said Yawen.

For a long time, there was no reply, but Ru'ah thought she heard Iddo cry. That must have hurt Iddo deeply, thought Ru'ah.

"Yes, Yawen, you are right. I do not know the tradition as you do. I meant no offense," cried Iddo.

"I will speak no more of this, we must trust in the Great Fire," Yawen said. Again, silence filled the temple. That seemed to be the end of the discussion. Ru'ah was still thirsty but decided it best not to disturb the priests at this point. She started to return to her room but stopped when she heard Yawen continue.

"Now on to the matter of Ru'ah."

"Yes, Ru'ah," said Iddo. "Was it completed?"

"It was," said Yawen. After another long pause he continued. "She did not take to it as I had hoped."

What did I not take to? Thought Ru'ah. Was he talking about the ritual? She had done everything as she had done the previous time.

She followed his instructions, even against her better judgment. She had wept before the Great Fire. Was that where she had gone wrong? She thought back to that moment. How could she not have wept, it was the most beautiful thing she had ever seen. She remembered that Yawen had not wept, but she thought it was because he had seen the Great Fire before.

"I had feared she would not," Iddo said. "I suppose it is time."

"Yes, tomorrow we will send her on," said Yawen.

Ru'ah head them move about, it sounded like the priests were rising from the meal table. Ru'ah had to make a dash back to her room so that she would not be seen. The last thing she wanted now was to be caught spying.

As Ru'ah lay back down on her sleeping pad, her mind played the conversation between Iddo and Yawen over and over again. What had the Wise Scout said that upset them so much? Why had Yawen been so harsh with Iddo? What has she done to deserve to be sent away?

As exhausted and drained as she was, tears started to pour once again. She had spent so much time thinking about what life would be like outside of the temple, but now the thought of being sent away terrified her.

She thought back over her life with the priests. She remembered the first time she failed to read the ritual correctly. She had been so embarrassed. Iddo found her hiding in a corner sometime later and just sat with her. She remembered that Iddo and Yawen had not been mad at her after that mistake, rather they performed the ritual again the next day so that she could get it right.

She remembered the time a few years back when there was a drought. Swarms of pilgrims came to the temple in order to pray to the Great Fire. Day after day, the priests performed rituals non-stop. She grew so exhausted that she could not even stand up. She remembered how the priests called for a break from the rituals for a full day. They were all able to get rest and prepare for the next wave of pilgrims.

Ru'ah thought back to all the meals she shared with Iddo and Yawen. They were not the warm, family gatherings like the meals at Yri and Beng's home, but she still looked back on them fondly.

Did Iddo and Yawen not feel the same? Had all of these years meant nothing to them? She was sure after the celebration that they truly cared for her, but perhaps she really was just one of the many enslaved people under their care.

Ru'ah's mind drifted back to her dream. Now more than ever she longed for the comfort of her mother's arms.

She thought once again to the ritual, the fear she felt being alone with Yawen. The strain of having half her head shaved, only to have the other half shaved a few days later. The smell of wine infused into her skin. If she had done something wrong in the ritual, she did not want to know what she should have done differently.

The strength she felt after the ritual suddenly returned to her. Something had changed within her. Maybe Iddo and Yawen were upset about the prince, maybe they were upset at her, upset enough to send her away. Maybe her mother was out there somewhere trying to find her. All of these thoughts and emotions swirled around her. This new strength channeled a new thought in her.

If Iddo and Yawen were going to send her away, and if her mother was out there somewhere, the answer was clear. She would gladly leave. She would leave as soon as she could say goodbye to Yri and Beng. She would find her mother.

Chapter Three

Ru'ah woke with a start. She didn't remember falling asleep but when she looked out her window the sun was high in the sky. Had Iddo and Yawen let her sleep in? The memories from last night came flooding back to her. Was this part of their plan? Letting her sleep in before sending her away forever? Well, I won't give them a chance to send me away, Ru'ah thought. I will leave before they even know I'm awake.

Ru'ah had decided to sneak away to Yri and Beng's house and beg them for help. Surly after she explained everything to them, they would be willing to give her enough food and water to survive in the desert. She hoped that Gand would also be willing to come with her, at least for a little while. As a scout, he knew the desert better than anyone else – maybe he would even know where the crop field would be.

With this plan in mind Ru'ah crept out of her room, trying hard to not make a sound.

But immediately her plan was foiled. Iddo and Yawen had been waiting for her all along.

"Ru'ah, come into the meal room," Iddo said as soon as she saw Ru'ah.

Having no choice but to obey, Ru'ah did as she was told. But she was fuming. She wanted to scream at them that she had heard their plan, that she knew she was going to be sent away. She wanted to curse them and the Great Fire. But at the thought of the Great Fire, she felt her blood turn cold. Something inside her told her to calm down and listen.

"We allowed you to sleep in this morning because there is something of great importance we need from you," Iddo continued.

"As you know, the pilgrims from Enst in the North have stopped coming to the temple because their prince has forbidden them to come. He insists on seeing the Great Fire himself, which, of course is unacceptable."

Ru'ah knew all of this but was taken aback at Iddo speaking so openly about it.

"It is our tradition since the time of the first Chief Priests that only the Chief Priests and the acolyte who is of age can know the Great Fire. That will continue to be the tradition forever," said Iddo. "It is so important that you understand that. Do you understand?" Iddo asked

Ru'ah's head was spinning at this, but she nodded her response.

Satisfied, Iddo continued, "This prince has caused a rift in this tradition. Since he is forbidding his people from coming to the temple, they cannot participate in the proper rituals to appease the Great Fire. This is of great concern to us. The Great Fire gives, and the Great Fire takes away. If the Great Fire is displeased it could take away from the people of the kingdom of Enst in the North. This would wreak havoc on the lives of this city and in the kingdom of Kal'i in the South. The Great Fire could become so displeased it might destroy us all. We have given our lives to satisfying the Great Fire, but now we must turn to you."

Ru'ah looked up at Iddo. Last night Iddo was planning to send her away, but now she was turning to her for help. What was going on, thought Ru'ah.

"We must send you into the desert in search of wick water. This is a blessed water that the Great Fire thrives on. We have not needed it in so long, yet now with the prince's threats we fear it may be the only thing that will save us," said Iddo.

Was this the answer? Had Ru'ah completely misunderstood what Iddo was saying the night before? She was not being sent away after all; she was being entrusted with a mission for the Great Fire. At this revelation, her whole demeanor changed. She sat up straighter in her chair.

Iddo and Yawen must have noticed because they exchanged a looked and Yawen took over speaking.

"This is of great importance, you understand. Iddo and I must stay here to continue the rituals. We must be able to trust that you will find the wick water and bring it back as quickly as possible."

"I understand, and I will," said Ru'ah.

Yawen and Iddo looked pleased.

"I once had to get wick water, many years ago," said Yawen. "I will tell you as much as I can about the way to go."

It had not occurred to Ru'ah that she did not know the way to go, she was just please with their trust in her. She was grateful that Yawen would show her at least where to begin the journey. She had been planning on running away just moments before, but now she was grateful she did not have to. However, there was one part of her plan this morning she hoped to keep.

"I will do this mission on my own, but I wonder if one of the scouts can lead me into the desert. Perhaps the scout Gand?" she asked almost in a whisper.

Yawen and Iddo exchanged another look.

"Gand can show you the way to begin, but it is crucial that you make this journey alone," Yawen said with a tone that told Ru'ah it was his final word on the matter.

"Let us eat our midday meal then make final preparations. You will leave first thing in the morning," Iddo said.

The three ate in the usual silence, yet with anticipation hanging in the air. She could feel that Yawen and Iddo were anxious for the wick water. She was anxious for the journey as well.

Once again after midday meal she found herself alone with Yawen. She wondered why Iddo was not with them this time but did not want to push Yawen with questions.

Yawen unfurled a map of the known world. She saw their city, Negev in the center. An ancient hand had crafted these fine markings. To the north was the Kingdom of Enst nestled in the high hills with the river running through it. To the south was Kal'i and its vast orchards. Where would this wick water be, Ru'ah wondered.

To answer her question, Yawen spoke, "You must go neither North nor South, but instead go West."

As he spoke, Yawen walked his fingers to the left of Negev. "Go as far west as you can," he continued. "Go west where there is nothing but sand, go as west as you can and when you can go no further there is an oasis. In the oasis there is a stream so pure and sweet, you can smell it before you can see it. That is the stream of the wick water. Take this vial to fill. This is the vial of the priests. No other vial can desecrate this sacred water. Do you understand?" asked Yawen.

Ru'ah nodded. The oasis was not on the map, it seemed it was outside the known world. How would she know if she was going the right direction?

She worked up the courage to ask Yawen.

"Follow the setting of the sun," he answered.

He folded up the map. Ru'ah had expected him to hand it over to her, but he did not. Instead, he dismissed her.

"Since this is my last night in the city before I leave, I would like to spend time with Yri and Beng," Ru'ah said as she made her way out of the room.

"Yes, I think that would be appropriate," said Yawen.

Ru'ah left before he could change his mind. She had so much she wanted to say to Yri. She ran to their home as fast as she could.

"Is everything ok?" Yri called out, holding the door open for Ru'ah.

"Yes, yes everything is ok, but I am going away first thing in the morning," replied Ru'ah.

"What? I don't understand, where are you going?" asked Yri.

Ru'ah realized that she might have said too much. She had been entrusted with the secret of the Great Fire and wick water, and she had already almost blurted it out.

Yri must have seen the hesitation on her face.

"Well, come in and catch your breath before you say anything else," said Yri.

Ru'ah came into the house and gathered her thoughts. What was it she could say to this family? Could she tell them about her mother? Her plan to run away? Her new mission?

To her relief Gand was there as well. As soon as he saw her, he said, "I hear I am to take you away in the morning."

"All right, someone better explain what is going on," interjected Beng.

Before Ru'ah could say anything else, Gand continued. "All I know is that the priest Iddo came to the scouts hut after midday meal and informed me that I would be starting Ru'ah on a journey tomorrow pointing west. I was told that was all the information I needed to know."

Ah, that's where Iddo had been when Yawen showed her the map, thought Ru'ah.

"This is what you were saying now? That the priests are sending you on a journey?" asked Yri.

"Yes, I can say no more than that, but I will be going first thing in the morning. That is why I have been allowed to come here, to say goodbye," Ru'ah said.

"Goodbye? How long will you be gone?" asked Yri.

Ru'ah saw that Yri looked genuinely concerned. She did not mean to upset her. She thought the family would be happy that the priests entrusted her.

"I will be gone as long as it takes," she said, without much confidence.

The room grew silent. No one really knew what to say next.

It was Beng who finally broke the silence.

"Well, we must make this a night to remember. I will get to work preparing the meal!"

The usual bustle began. Gand went to help Beng in the kitchen. Ru'ah looked around at this loving home. She suddenly realized what leaving would mean.

"Ru'ah it is an honor for you to be sent on this journey, I'm sure, but I will deeply miss you," Yri said as she sat down.

"Yes, I will miss you all too. I will return as quickly as I can," Ru'ah replied choking down tears.

"Is there something else?" Yri asked with concern in her voice.

"I saw her," Ru'ah whispered.

"Saw who?" asked Yri.

"My mother."

Yri did not say anything for a long time.

"Ru'ah I have never known you to have a mother," she finally said.

"I saw her, last night. She came to me in a dream." Ru'ah told Yri. "But it was more than a dream, it felt so real. She was there with me."

"Ru'ah, it was a dream," said Yri.

"I know, but she was there. She's out there somewhere!" said Ru'ah.

Yri became more concerned. "Is that what your journey is? To find your mother? Is that where the priests are sending you?"

"No," admitted Ru'ah. "But I hope that maybe on the way I can find her."

"Ru'ah I urge you do not go down this path," said Yri.

Now it was Ru'ah who became concerned. Why was Yri being unsupportive of her finding her mother? Yri didn't know what it was like to be without family. How could she? The more Ru'ah thought about it, the angrier she became.

She was just about to admonish Yri when Gand barged back into the room.

"We have done it," he announced. "We have created a meal worthy of the acolyte. Everyone come and let us eat!"

The evening meal was a little more delicious than usual. Maybe it was the amount of love that went into it, but Ru'ah savored every bite. She delighted in the stories that were told, even the ones she had heard many times before. Her heart grew heavy thinking about not seeing this family for a long time. How many times had she eaten with them? How many nights had she longed to be with them instead of alone in her room? How many times did Yri and Beng come to her rescue? This journey was hers to take, but she started to realize it did not come without sacrifice.

Ru'ah's thoughts were interrupted by the chorus of children begging her to tell them one last temple story before Beng sent them home.

"I do have one last story," she said to them, "but it is not a temple story. Would you like to hear it anyway?"

"Yes!" they all cheered.

"Out in the middle of the vast desert there is a field of crop that smells so sweet," she began. All eyes were on her; all ears were hanging on her every word.

"The crop field goes on for miles and miles, it is an endless oasis. And in the middle of the crop field is the sweetest voice ever heard.

The voice speaks truths to all who listen. The voice knows the number of the stars in the sky. And I have heard this voice myself."

The children leaned in closer, mesmerized by what would happen next.

Ru'ah continued, "this voice is a voice that I love; this voice is the voice of my mother!"

"Your mother?" the children asked, "Tell us about her!"

"She is the most beautiful women in the world. And she is out there waiting for me," Ru'ah trailed off.

The children jumped up and down asking her more questions, but she did not hear any of it. Her mind had wandered to that field out in the desert. She prayed to the Great Fire that she would find it on the way to the wick water. She prayed her mother would come back to the city with her.

The children grew restless with her lack of response. Beng gathered them up and told them to say one last goodbye to their dear friend. One by one, she gave them big hugs and said goodnight. She sent out another prayer that she would see them all again soon.

Yri and Beng left to take the children home for the evening and Ru'ah realized she was alone with Gand.

"That was some story," he said to her.

"Yes, it is my new favorite story," she replied.

Ru'ah noticed Gand did not meet her eye, as if he was trying to hide something from her. She did not know what else to say.

Finally, Yri came back into the room. "Would it be all right if I walked you back, at least to the tree?" she asked Ru'ah.

How could she refuse? She wanted to spend as much time with Yri as possible.

As the two women walked together into the night Ru'ah thought about the last time they did this. Was it really only a few days ago? It seemed like a lifetime.

"I did not mean to upset you," Yri said interrupting the silence of the night. "I know you think you saw your mother, but Ru'ah it was just a dream."

"Yri, you have to believe me, it was more than a dream, I know she's out there waiting for me," Ru'ah begged Yri to understand.

"You know I've always looked at you at one of my own children. Beng and I have tried to take care of you as much as we can all these years. I know life in the temple is very difficult for you," Yri said.

"Please do not be jealous," said Ru'ah. "I love you and Beng so much and will always think of you as my family. But my mother is my mother."

"I do not want our last night together to be spoiled by a fight. I am just worried for you," said Yri.

"There is no need to worry; Gand will show me the way. I trust that the priests have given me good guidance and will provide enough supplies for the journey," said Ru'ah.

"I know you will be prepared on the journey," said Yri. Ru'ah could see she was still worried but decided not to push the topic. She did not want to spoil the evening with a fight either.

Then the two approached the tree and stood for a long time in each other's company. Again, Ru'ah's heart grew heavy thinking about the next time they would be together. It could indeed be a very long time from now.

The night grew darker and darker, finally Yri had to say goodbye. Ru'ah wiped a tear off her cheek as she hugged Yri.

"I promise I will be safe, and I will be back soon," she said.

"I know, and I love you," Yri said.

The two parted ways, Yri back to her home and family, Ru'ah to a journey unknown.

When Ru'ah returned to her room, she looked out her window over the only city she had ever known. She looked up into the stars and thought about her mother once again. She thought about the wick water and the Great Fire. So many things in her life were counting on her success.

Exhausted and overwhelmed she lay down to a dreamless sleep.

The next morning, she was awoken with the rising sun by Iddo calling her name. At first, she thought about the usual morning chores she needed to get done, but remembered that today was no ordinary day. She looked up at Iddo who was beckoning her to come out into the Realm.

"Before you leave, we must perform the ritual. Let us eat first in haste, there is not much time to lose," Iddo said.

Just as was said, the priests and Ru'ah ate quickly then returned to the Realm.

Yawen had Ru'ah stand before the altar once again. Instead of laying down Iddo gestured for her to kneel. Ru'ah was grateful this was not the same ritual she had gone through at her coming of age. Instead, Iddo and Yawen poured oil over her and chanted a blessing. She also said a silent prayer to the Great Fire for safety and for her mother.

The three left the Realm in silence and descended the great stairs. When they arrived at the bottom, Yawen led her to a pack that had been pre-filled.

"This is the amount of supplies I had when I went to gather wick water many years ago. I trust this will be enough for you as well," he said.

Ru'ah did not argue. She pulled the pack onto her back and folded over at the weight of it.

"You will grow stronger as you walk and the pack will grow lighter," said Yawen as a way of encouragement.

After a few minutes of struggle, Ru'ah was able to situate the pack in a way that made it manageable. She slowly walked on, following Iddo and Yawen to the scout's hut.

Both Tell and Gand were waiting for them.

"Ru'ah, it is with our greatest trust in you that we send you out to begin your journey with Gand," Tell announced. "We trust that you will return safely when the time is right." Tell then gave Ru'ah a scout's salute. She felt very honored indeed.

She began to follow Tell and Gand out of the city but felt a hand on her shoulder. She turned back to Iddo and Yawen.

"This is your journey that you must take," said Yawen.

Ru'ah nodded and turned to Iddo to say goodbye but, to her surprise, Iddo was looking hard at the ground.

Once again, she turned to leave, this time the priests did not stop her.

She walked out of the city gates and looked at the vastness of the desert. She had seen it from her room, but never this close before. The dunes spread on for miles and miles. She thought how easy it would be to get lost. Just follow the setting of the sun, she thought to herself.

"Gand will go with you until the first sun set, then he must return," Tell said as Ru'ah joined them. "I can offer you no further help; you will be on your own."

"I thank you for allowing Gand to go with me even for a little while," Ru'ah said before Tell went back to the scout's hut.

Ru'ah and Gand stood together looking out into the desert.

"Shall we begin?" Ru'ah asked as she took her first step of the journey.

"Ru'ah wait, there is something I must say first," said Gand.

He looked deeply at her but hesitated. What could Gand need to say that was causing him to fluster like that? The look he gave her was one of deep care and concern.

"Ru'ah I have to tell you before you go that I have been scouting this desert since I came of age a few years back. I have been up to Enst in the North and down to Kal'i in the South. I have been as west as I can go and so Ru'ah I have to tell you … there is no crop field in the desert."

Ru'ah was taken aback. She did not know what Gand was going to say, but she was not expecting that.

"Maybe it's further out that you have ever been," she finally mumbled.

"Ru'ah, the desert is a hard and unforgiving place. It is barren outside of the kingdoms. The only way this city survives is because of the gifts given by the pilgrims. Do you understand?" said Gand.

"I know what I saw, and I know my mother is out there," she replied, this time with a stronger voice.

Why was Gand being so insistent? Had Yri put him up to this? Why couldn't they understand how important it was for her to find her mother?

"I want you to be safe, I want you to come back," Gand said, something in his voice had changed. It was softer, almost pleading.

"I must begin my journey," Ru'ah said.

Ru'ah walked with Gand out into the desert leaving behind Negev, the Great Fire, the priests, and all she had ever known.

They stopped at midday to see what provisions they had for a meal. Gand looked inside her pack.

"Wow, you really do have enough in here for a long journey. The priests knew what they were doing," he said pulling out some bread and water. "I never took them for desert travelers."

"Yawen said he took this journey once before and knew what I would need," Ru'ah said. She immediately regretted saying anything. Was that part of the secret of the journey?

As if reading her mind, Gand said, "Don't worry. Your secret is safe with me."

After the short meal break was over, Gand showed Ru'ah how to cover herself to protect against the heat of the day.

"I wish you could come with me the whole way," Ru'ah said absentmindedly.

"As do I, if only to protect you from yourself," Gand said with a wink.

Ru'ah was grateful for the company but knew it would be short lived. The two continued to walk and talk long into the afternoon. He told stories of his childhood she had never heard before. She did not say much, but enjoyed listening to him. He did not seem to mind talking.

Before they knew it, the sun was starting to set and Gand would have to return home. For the first time since learning about the journey, Ru'ah felt a tinge of fear.

"I fear it is time for us to part," Gand said. "Do you know the way?"

"Follow the setting of the sun," Ru'ah whispered. Then she surprised herself by jumping into his arms. He held her for as long as he could.

"I fear I really must go, I do not want to worry the Wise Scout, or the priests for that matter," Gand said.

"I will return soon," Ru'ah said as she let him go.

Away he went back towards the city. She watched him until she could see him no more.

As the night air grew colder, she unpacked another piece of bread to eat and some water to drink. Gand was right that there were many provisions in her pack. She had no idea how long they would last, but she tried not to think about it. It was so quiet out in the desert. No birds sang their evening songs, no dogs barked for a scrap of food, not even an insect flapped its wings around her. This was true silence.

Ru'ah's mind drifted back to Negev. She wondered what the priests were up to this night. Perhaps they were performing a ritual for her. She thought of the Great Fire and its warmth. She tried to draw strength from just the memory of it. She thought back to Yri and Beng. She hoped Gand was making a safe journey home.

One by one, the stars twinkled above her. She counted them as their lights grew stronger. But, she still could not keep track, there were just too many.

My mother knows how many, she thought to herself.

She drew a blanket around herself to keep the chill away. Alone in the dark of the desert, she fell asleep still trying to count the stars.

The next morning, she woke up with a start. As cold as she had been last night, she was now quite warm. She looked around and noticed the sun was well into the sky.

"Follow the setting of the sun," she said to herself. "If the sun sets in the west, I must start walking away from where it rises." Once again, she pulled out food and water from her bag to start the day.

"I wonder how long this will last, and how long I can last on it," she said to herself, realizing that it was mostly bread and water in her pack.

When she had satisfied her hunger once more, she sat back out on her journey.

The first few days passed without much concern. Ru'ah had no idea how long she walked, she just knew she had to keep walking. While she walked, she kept her eyes peeled for any sign of an oasis. At one point, she thought she spotted one in the distance, but as she got closer, she realized it was only a mirage. Her eyes were already starting to play tricks on her. That was not a good sign, she thought.

That night she lay down once more under the stars. She was hungry and thirsty but feared to eat and drink any more than absolutely necessary. There was nothing but desert all around as far as the eye could see. She needed her supplies to last to the oasis and on the journey back.

"How did Yawen do this?" Ru'ah said. "He claims this was all the supplies he needed, but that was a long time ago. Maybe he had help too."

She was becoming afraid of this journey. She thought once more to the Great Fire.

Then she did something that surprised herself, she started talking to the Great Fire as if it were there with her.

"Great Fire, I think I need help," she said. "I know this is my journey to take, but I am not sure what to do. I will follow the setting of the sun, but I am only human. Please help me if you can."

Ru'ah felt a little silly saying this, but she couldn't think of anything else to do. She wanted so badly to return to Negev, to Yri and Beng and Gand. She did not want to fail, but she didn't know if she could do this after all.

Like the night before, when the stars came out, she thought about her mother. Maybe my mother can help, she thought.

"Mother I know you are out there. Will you help me?" she called out.

Silence answered her. Once more, she drew the blanket around her as the chill in the air grew stronger. Unlike last night, though, there was a sudden gust of wind. All around her, the sand swirled. The wind grew stronger and stronger picking up speed. Instinct kicked in and she lay low to the ground. Just as quickly as it had started, the wind once again died down and the sand settled.

But, a whisper remained. As if there were someone next to her, Ru'ah heard her name being called.

"Ru'ah" came the voice in the wind.

"Mother?" Ru'ah called back. She listened for a response, but none came.

"Mother, are you out there?" Ru'ah called again. Nothing but silence.

"Mother, I will find you," she called one last time.

Ru'ah lay back down under the stars once more. She started to count them one by one.

"I will find you mother," she whispered before falling asleep once more.

Once again Ru'ah was awoken by the rays of the sun in the early morning. She was beginning to feel the monotony of the days. Everything was the same for miles around her. No sound, no sight other than sand, and certainly no other people. She had grown used be being lonely, but she had never before been so alone.

She set up in the sand and coughed the dust away. "Maybe today will be the day I find the oasis," Ru'ah said to herself. "Maybe today will be the day I find my mother."

She rummaged through her pack for a piece of bread and water before starting her journey. She was trying so hard to parse out her supplies, but it was getting harder and harder. "What I wouldn't do for fresh bread baked by Caff, or a meal prepared by Beng."

This thought of home made her pause and sit back down. She needed just a little more time this morning before she set out again.

As Ru'ah let her mind wonder back over the past few days she absentmindedly let her bread slip out of her hand and into the sand. She only realized what had happened when she felt tiny pricks on her legs and feet. Looking down she realized that an army of insects had come out of nowhere to collect this small offering of bread.

At first, she was fascinated by them. They were the first living creatures she had come across since Gand left. They were curious little creatures. One by one, they gathered the biggest morsels they could from the larger piece. Then the scurried back into the sand. She stared in awe of them for several minutes.

She became fond of them and felt for their struggle to survive in the desert, so she decided she could spare a little bit more bread for them. Grabbing another handful, she tossed more into their path. The frenzy made her laugh. "Look how they run around. This might be the only meal they have for a while," she thought.

Then something strange happened. These insects, desperate for this new source of food, became possessive. The larger ones would gather more and more food, leaving less for the stragglers. Then, to her horror, they started stealing morsels from one another. "Should I give them more food, so they all have enough?" she thought. She knew she couldn't spare too much more bread or else she wouldn't have enough for herself.

As she watched, the scene became more and more violent. The insects had become so possessive over the food they started fighting and killing one another over it. After only a few moments, all the bread had been claimed. The ones who won the fights had disappeared back into the sand while only the dead bodies of the others remained.

Ru'ah had heard tale of animals having to fight for their survival, but this was the first time she had seen it up close. She hoped she would never have to see anything like that again.

She gathered up her pack and left once more on her journey. "At least there are other living creatures in the desert," she thought. "That means there are ways to survive."

She did not have to go far before she saw the next sign of life. By midday, she came across an oasis. She knew it was not the one she had been looking for since, really, it was only a small puddle. Perhaps it had rained recently, and this was the remnants. Either way, she was grateful for the chance to refill her pack with fresh water.

She was just about to reach into her pack when she noticed another curious sight. Three small mouse-like creatures were floating in the puddle. None of them were alive anymore.

What had killed them? She thought to herself. She knew she would need more water, but should she chance this water? What if there was something wrong with it that had killed these creatures? Was it worth the risk? She decided to sit by the puddle to see if any other animals would come and drink from it.

She sat quietly there for the rest of the day. She knew she should keep going to get to her oasis, but she was quickly losing hope.

Fear had long ago left her; she now only cared about survival. Yawen was right, the pack was getting lighter and easier to carry, but she knew that meant she was running out of supplies.

She stayed the night by the puddle without seeing another living thing. The next morning, she had to force herself to keep going. One step at a time, one step at a time she said to herself. To pass the time she tried to remember songs and rhymes from her childhood but soon her mind could focus on nothing but the sand in front of her.

"Perhaps Gand will come looking for me soon," she thought. Although she knew he wouldn't. Yawen was very clear that she had to do this on her own, and the scouts would never disobey him, no matter how Gand felt about her.

She was even starting to lose hope of finding her mother. Where would she even be out here, there was nothing but sand all around. She could not be surviving all on her own. By the time the sun was setting that day she felt more desperate than ever.

"I have failed. I have failed this mission, I have failed the priests, and I have failed the Great Fire."

She could no longer remember the temple. Everything before the desert was a blur. She tried to think about Yri and Beng but could hardly remember their faces. She tried to think about Iddo and Yawen but felt nothing but anger towards them now. They had sent her on this journey; they had left her all on her own.

That night, instead of looking up at the stars, all she could think about were the insects and how they were so desperate to survive that they killed one another. Could it be possible for humans to do that too? Could it be possible that this was Iddo and Yawen's plan all along?

She could not bear that thought, but it was her last thought before she drifted off into a restless sleep.

That night she dreamed she was once again surrounded by fire. There were no crops this time and her mother was no where to be found, there was only fire. In her dream she called out for help, and no one answered. She begged and pleaded with the Great Fire to save her, but once again was met with nothing. In her dream, she become more and more desperate until she finally succumbed to the flames. She awoke with the flames of the burning sun on her.

She knew that had just been a dream, but it left her with an even deeper sense of abandonment. Ever since Gand had left, she had faced nothing but sand and sun and death. She rummaged through her pack and realized just how little food and water she had left.

She had seen no signs of an oasis and had no hope of finding it any time soon. She was hotter than she had ever been and hungrier than she had ever been. Even standing took more effort than she could muster. She tried eating but found she could not make herself chew. There was not enough water in the world that would satisfy her. She had reached the end of her rope.

She looked all around for something to grasp, something that would help her to go on, but there was nothing. Is this how it would end for her, out here alone in the desert? Had Iddo and Yawen sent her to her death? Maybe she should have run away after all.

"Mother, I wanted so badly to find you. I tried," she cried out in desperation.

Something inside broke at that moment and she was no longer sad or afraid, instead she was angry. Angry that she was ever made acolyte in the first place, angry that she had been so fascinated with the Great Fire – the Great Fire was the reason Iddo and Yawen sent her to her death after all. She was angry at Yri and Beng for not doing more to help her – but what could they do? Surly they could have done something. She was angry at Gand for leaving her out here all alone. If he cared for her at all, he would have gone with her, despite any orders he must obey.

Ru'ah was so angry that her rage flew out of her in the form of tears. She cried harder than she had ever cried before. While she cried, she started to curse Iddo and Yawen. She cursed the Great Fire. She cursed that united couple from all those years ago who became the first priests of the Great Fire.

"Curse you all!" She shouted out into the empty desert.

She did not deserve this; she did not deserve to die all alone. She deserved to be loved, that was all she ever wanted. She deserved happiness and a life of her own.

"Curse you!" she called out one more time before dissolving totally into tears. She cried until she had no more strength, she cried until she collapsed into the desert sand. She cried and cried, and planned to cry until she died.

Instead, she fell asleep. She did not know how long she had been asleep, but the sun was still hot on her back when she woke up. She gathered what was left of her strength. She would sit up, eat and drink what she could and then decide what to do next. As she sat up, she realized that she was no longer alone.

She looked around and instead of sand, she was surrounded, totally and completely, by a field of crops that had the sweetest smell.

Chapter Four

Ru'ah could not believe her eyes. She even pinched herself to see if she was actually awake and not dreaming. After so long wondering in the desert, she couldn't be sure this wasn't just a mirage, or worse. Was she wake but imagining this? This is what she had been looking for, but was it real? She reached out to touch one of the pods that hung right about her. It was firm to the touch, but she easily plucked it off the stalk.

What kind of crop was this after all? She was not familiar with it outside of her dream, and it was unlike any she had ever seen. Was this the crop from her dream? It looked the same and smelled the same. It must be. After a few moments, curiosity got the better of her. Ru'ah peeled back the rough exterior of the pod. Inside, a hue of deep purple welcomed her. She pulled the pod off and held the remains in her hand. It felt almost like a peach – soft but not delicate. Its purple color was as vibrant as a gem. It smelled even more delicious now that the pod had been removed. After a few moments of admiration, she plopped it into her mouth. It was a fruit unlike any other she had tasted. Sweet and filling. All her hunger and thirst vanished instantly. Her mind was alive once more.

This had to be the crop from her dream! That meant her mother must be nearby.

Ru'ah shot up from the ground and started running down the winding path. Surly she would be here somewhere.

"Mother! Mother!" she called out as she ran.

The field was as large as she remembered. She ran, it seemed, for miles and miles. The sweet smell filled her lungs and gave her a boost of energy. She stopped every once in a while to taste another piece of the fruit. Each bite was better than the last.

Ru'ah's joy was palpable as she continued running through the maze.

"Mother, Mother" she continued to call. She must be here, she thought to herself.

At last, she could run no more. She sat back down under the shade of the tall crops to catch her breath. This was the most amazing thing she could ever dream of. But, how? How did the crop just show up? The answer gnawed at the back of her mind. She knew why but couldn't bring herself to believe it. The crop showed up because of her. It was as if her tears brought it out of the ground just for her. She did not know why, but she knew this crop had just saved her life.

And it would seem the crops were doing more than saving her life. She looked down at the ground once again to see those same insects she had seen just a few days before. But this time they were not fighting to the death. One by one, they were climbing up the stalks to gather this fruit for themselves. There was clearly enough food now to go around.

Once again, her mind wandered to where her mother might be. Perhaps I should stay in one place so she can find me, thought Ru'ah.

The sun grew hot in the sky, but Ru'ah did not feel overwhelmed by the heat for the first time since her journey began. She knew she would be safe and protected here, at least for now.

The day dragged on. Ru'ah had grown used to being alone out in the desert. Walking helped the time go by without much notice, but now that she was alone and did not have th3 distractions of hunger and thirst, she wasn't sure what to do.

She would get up to walk around, then sit back down. Get up, sit back down. Eventually the sun began to go down. Follow the setting of the sun, she thought to herself. Perhaps I should move on and continue looking for the oasis, she thought. But she wasn't ready to leave, not yet. Her mother would show up soon, she knew it.

As the stars twinkled in the sky, she lay down once again to sleep. Maybe tomorrow would bring what she was waiting for.

She dreamed peaceful dreams now that she had nourishment once more. She dreamed of the stars dancing all around her. She dreamed of a deep and cool pool of water that she could bathe in. She dreamed of that most beautiful voice calling her name, "Ru'ah … Ru'ah …"

She awoke bright and early the next morning. She ate once more of the sweet fruit that surrounded her. It was all she had eaten for the past day and yet she was still not sick of it. She wondered if she would ever be; it was so delicious.

The morning went by without much incident. She continued her pattern of getting up for a while then sitting back down for a while.

"I cannot keep this up for much longer," she said out loud. She was determined to keep herself busy so that she would not feel the need to move on.

"Perhaps I can make myself a shelter," she decided.

Ru'ah had never built a shelter before; she never had any need to. This would be the perfect time to learn.

She looked around at the stalks. They looked sturdy enough to hold up to any wind. She would need to figure out how to secure them to one another. She looked in her pack. She did not have much as far as rope went, so she would have to fashion something together. Really, the only options were her blanket and the clothes on her back. Since she had been comfortable enough without it last night, she decided to use her blanket.

Ru'ah carefully tore the blanket into shreds. Her idea was to use the shreds to tie the tops of the stalks together to form a primitive hut. She thought back to the scout's hut. Hers would be nowhere near as advanced as theirs was, but it would be better than nothing.

Once she was satisfied with the blanket shreds, the next step was figuring out how to reach the top of the stalks. They were all several feet higher than she was. She didn't think climbing them was an option. She thought instead of how to bend them down to her level to tie the shred of blanket on. She reached up to the stalks and was amazed at how malleable they were. It was almost as if they were answering to her hand. Her plan worked. Soon she had what could pass as a shelter. She had reached her other goal of making the time go by as well. She could tell by the position of the sun in the sky that it was several hours later.

She tried to be humble in her life, but she couldn't help but he proud of what she had accomplished. No, her shelter was not nearly as nice or advanced as the scout's hut, but she had made it by herself, with her own hands.

To celebrate she ate more fruit and took a midday nap in her handmade hut.

When she awoke, there was still no sign of her mother. But Ru'ah was resolved to not simply sit and wait. She could make a shelter all by herself, what else could she do? What else was there to do?

She looked around and saw nothing but crop. Maybe that was the answer. She would find out what all this crop was good for. Of course, she knew it was good for food. She thought back to Negev and the market vendors. They did not wait for food to show up to them, they gathered the food for themselves. That's what she would do. She would spend time collecting the fruit off the stalk so that she would have it readily available.

Ru'ah emptied her pack of the leftover bread and water. She was shocked at how little there was left. She really only had a few days' worth until it would have run out. Did Yawen really expect her to survive on that? Or, was that his plan? She tried not to think about that for too long.

She did not want to get rid of the bread and water. Instead, she lay them in a corner of her shelter to save for another time. It took longer than expected to fill her pack with fruit. She would pull them from the stalk, take them out of the pod and place them in her bag. Over and over it went. Occasionally she would enjoy a snack as well. She was pleased that the sun was going down once more when her pack was finally full. Instinct told her to dig a hole in her shelter to bury the fruit. This would keep it cool and safe. After all that, the stars were shining brightly in the sky. It was time for sleep. She would continue her mission tomorrow.

When she woke up, she thought she would be sore from the labor of the previous day; instead she was energized. She had done all of those things herself and wanted to keep doing things for herself. She loved not having to follow orders from the priests. She loved that she could do what she wanted when she wanted.

Ru'ah did think of Yri and Beng. They never spoke ill of the priests, but she knew they too longed for freedom. Everyone in Negev was enslaved to Iddo and Yawen. Everyone did as they were told. Perhaps everyone would have loved their own freedom like Yri and Beng wanted, like Ru'ah had now. She wished she could share this freedom with her city. But how? Maybe one day she would figure it out.

But for now, she could not leave the crop field, her mother had still not shown up. Back to the crop itself. When she was gathering fruit the previous day, she had decided that the next thing she wanted to learn about was the stalk. She had found out it was malleable enough to make a shelter, but what else could it do?

Ru'ah went to pull a stalk about of the ground but froze. Was she allowed to do this after all? The crop had shown up for her, but did that mean she could pull it out of the ground? She knew enough about plants to know that pulling it up would mean that it died. She did not want to do that to this precious crop. Instead, she looked at the leaves. They were long, for the size of the crop, and quite soft. Perhaps she could use them to replace the blanket she had shredded the day before.

She gathered up as many of the leaves as she felt comfortable with and headed back to sit in her hut. She had spent enough time working with fabrics with Yri to know the basics of weaving. As she worked the leaves, she was pleased with how easy it was. Like the stalks, they seemed to obey her hands and her mind. It was empowering to watch these leaves turn into the blanket she hoped they would be. Again, she felt proud that she had created something all by herself.

She decided to spend the rest of the day using the leaves to make new clothes. She didn't mind only having one outfit, but she had been out in the desert with no change of clothes for some time now. How long had she been out here, she thought? She honestly couldn't remember – it was all a blur.

As night drew in, she fell asleep with the peace that comes after a day's work. And, it was work she wanted to do for herself.

Ru'ah spent the next few days exploring the field. She felt confident that she knew her way around. But since it was a maze, so she never went too far at once. Every day she would spend some time looking for her mother, but she had not shown up yet. Ru'ah kept herself busy with harvesting the crop, keeping up with her small hut and learning all kinds of new skills. She had discovered in her pack a small knife. Maybe Yawen gave it to her so she could protect herself but had forgotten to tell her.

When she discovered it, she spent hours teaching herself how to throw it accurately. I'm becoming quite the survivalist, she thought to herself. She was pleased this was the case because she did not know how much longer she would have to be out there. The days were once again starting to blur together. How long had she been there already?

She had at least been out there long enough to have started a routine. Ru'ah woke every morning with the sun. She had gotten used to waking up early in the temple, but it was nice to be able to choose to wake up that early instead of being called upon by the priests. She would then eat a morning meal of a few pieces of fruit and spend the rest of the morning patrolling the field to see if there were any signs of her mother. Midday meal consisted of more fruit followed by a nap in the shade of her hut. She loved the way the wind blew against skin in the open air. The afternoon consisted of maintenance of her tools, and hut. She was becoming proficient with her knife, and thankful Yawen had included it in her pack.

Somehow, she had not become bored yet. She was also amazed that she was able to survive on the fruit alone. Even her thirst was satisfied by it. This really was a miracle crop. She was still lonely, but she took joy in living life on her own terms for the first time ever. And she held on to the notion that her mother would show up soon enough.

Days, weeks, months maybe, had gone by. She did not know exactly. Ru'ah was on her usual patrol one morning when she felt a change in the air. She usually didn't wander too far from her hut but this morning something was drawing her out. She could sense that something needed her attention. She walked and walked on through the crop field. Like a magnet being pulled to iron. On and on, further than she had been in a long time until finally she found that she had made her way out of the field altogether.

Immediately she felt exposed. The sky was brighter, the sun warmer, the desert vast. She did not have the comfort and protection she was used to. She went to turn back, to run, but stopped in her tracks. There was a voice.

"Hello!"

This voice rang loud and clear over the desert. She had been waiting so long for a voice to come to her. But not this voice. This was not the beautiful voice she knew from her dream. This was different, harsher; unfamiliar.

"Hello," the voice came again.

Ru'ah turned around to see where the voice was coming from. She did not have to look far. Right in front of her stood a warrior. He was tall and broad enough to block out the sun. His hair was dark brown and his skin, bronze. She recognized the insignia on his pack. He was of the noble house of the Kingdom of Enst in the North. She had seen that insignia many times before when the warriors from Enst would come to the temple city for a blessing. But why was he out here?

"Hello," Ru'ah replied still trying to figure out what was happening.

The warrior must have expected Ru'ah to say something else because he remained silent for a moment.

"Who are you?" he finally asked.

"I am no one," said Ru'ah not willing to give up her identity to this stranger.

"No one? Really, and is this not your crop field?" asked the warrior. Ru'ah did not like the way he looked at the crop.

"This is my field, at least as much as it is anyone's," she replied.

"But you are no one, not anyone," the warrior said with a glint in his eye.

Ru'ah was starting to find her courage again. Why should she be scared? This was her field after all not his. He should be afraid of her.

"And who are you?" Ru'ah said with a strong voice.

"Aratam, of the house of Enst, the Kingdom of the North," the warrior proudly proclaimed.

"And what are you doing here?" Ru'ah asked.

"I have been sent by the prince to find a more direct route to Kal'i, the kingdom of the South. I had been traveling for many days when I stumbled upon the strangest sight I have ever seen – a crop field in the middle of the desert."

Ru'ah was taken aback. She had not expected to hear this. She was reminded of her original mission to find the wick water for the great fire. Did the warrior's presence here mean she had already failed?

"Why are you in need of a more direct path?" she finally asked.

"And why exactly would no one need to know the answer to that?" Aratam asked her.

Ru'ah had been caught. She could ignore his question and leave him alone, but she needed to know this news of the outside world.

"I am not no one, my name is Ru'ah. I am the acolyte to the Chief Priests Iddo and Yawen of the temple city Negev."

This time, it was Aratam who was taken aback. Ru'ah noticed for the first time he looked something other than smug.

"Why is the acolyte of the Chief Priests of the Great Fire in a mystery crop field in the middle of the desert," he asked in almost a whisper.

"That is a long story," Ru'ah replied.

"Then it is a good thing I am in need of a rest. Perhaps you could spare some shade for this humble messenger and maybe even some of this crop," he said, back to his strong voice.

Ru'ah stared at him for a long time. She was not sure if she was ready to share her crop with anyone, let alone someone who just showed up. But, once again, something inside her spoke to her, telling her she should extend this kindness to him. Against her better judgement, she agreed and led him through the long walk to her hut. She was grateful she remembered the way back.

Ru'ah was also grateful that Aratam walked in silence, she still wasn't sure how to respond to him. When they arrived at her hut, she gestured for him to have a seat outside. She uncovered her harvest but brought him only a handful.

Aratam looked hard at the fruit. Ru'ah watched him as he picked it up, examined it and finally plopped a piece in his mouth. He must have enjoyed it as much as she did because he had the same reaction to it.

"This is amazing," he said after another mouthful. "I've never had anything like it."

Ru'ah felt a surge of pride that someone else was enjoying her fruit so much. But that feeling was short lived, he was a still a stranger after all.

"All right warrior, tell me the whole story," she said.

"Ha! I am no warrior," Aratam laughed.

"You wear the warrior insignia of the Kingdom of Enst," Ru'ah insisted.

"Ah, that is where you are mistaken. This is not warrior insignia. This is the insignia all enslaved people of Enst must wear. I am a slave of the prince. I do his bidding, whatever that might be. And right now, his bidding is for me to find a more direct path between the kingdoms of Enst and Kal'i.

It made sense that Enst and Kal'i would also have people who were enslaved, but Ru'ah had never thought about that before. She thought that all who came to the temple city came of their own accord. It never occurred to her they may also be under orders from someone else.

"Why does the prince want a more direct route? Is it because the Chief Priests would not let him see the Great Fire for himself?" Ru'ah asked.

"Ah, so you are who you say you are. Yes, that is my understanding. Trading between Enst in the North and Kal'i in the South usually happens in the temple city," Aratam said. That surprised Ru'ah as well, since she did not know that was happening.

Aratam continued, "When your priests refused my prince an audience with the Great Fire, he decided he did not need the temple city after all. Instead, he would find his own route to the south, cutting out Negev altogether."

Ru'ah thought long and hard about what Aratam had just said. Her mind was still reeling from his very presence there at all, now he was telling her his prince wanted to cut out Negev. What would the priests say? As far as she knew, the two kingdoms had relied on the temple city since they were established, and the temple city relied on the two kingdoms bringing offerings. All the people of Negev relied on them for money to buy food and clothing, not just the priests. Ru'ah then thought an even worse thought: What would the kingdom of Enst do without the rituals to the Great Fire? In fact, she was in the desert to get the wick water to satisfy the Great Fire for this very reason. She had failed her mission after all. Would this mean death and destruction for all people? The prince could not do that, not to his own people, not to the people of Kal'i, and certainly not to the people of her own city. This was too much to bear.

"You mustn't, please for the sake of the Great Fire, please do not do this!' Ru'ah pleaded with Aratam.

"I am sorry, I must obey my orders," Aratam said with sympathy in his voice.

"Why is the prince doing this? Does he really want to see the Great Fire so badly?" Ru'ah said almost to herself.

The two sat in silence. Ru'ah knew that Aratam was bound by his master, just as she had been. She hadn't been free long enough to forget how powerful that bind was. She might never be, it was that strong.

Ru'ah was surprised when Aratam started speaking again. "My master is a greedy ruler," he said. "He was raised in luxury and has never experienced want. He takes and takes, without much thought. We in the kingdom of Enst honor the Great Fire, of course, but my master started to question why. He asked any and every one, his parents, the servants, even our local priests, why we should be paying homage to this Great Fire. No one could give him an answer that satisfied him. He went to the Chief Priests to see for himself why this Great Fire was so great. When they refused him, he decided, then and there, to punish the temple city. If he could not be satisfied, then he would do everything in his power to bring woe to those who were unsatisfactory. And that is why I have been sent on this mission."

Ru'ah heard the sadness in Aratam's voice. She looked at him again. He was not as he had first appeared. His face was not chiseled, but soft. He reminded her somewhat of Gand, hard around the edges, but kind.

"Do you like being a slave to your master?" she asked him.

"Ha! I have never met anyone who likes being a slave," Aratam said. "I do not like it, but it is my life. Did you like being a slave to your masters?" he asked her back.

Ru'ah had to think about how to answer that. Aratam was right, she did not like it; it was just her life.

"No, I suppose not," she finally answered. "They were kind to me, but ultimately they were my masters and I had to obey them."

"Yes," Aratam agreed. "So, why are you here now?" he asked after a pause.

"Now that is a long story," Ru'ah said.

Ru'ah told Aratam about everything. Her life as an acolyte, her coming of age celebration and ritual. She told him about Yri, Beng, and Gand. She told him about what she knew of his prince, she even told him about her journey to get the wick water. Finally, she told him about her dream of her mother and the crop field. She found he was quite easy to talk to; in fact, she rather enjoyed sharing these things with him.

"When I broke down crying, the crops surrounded me. I knew this was the crop field from my dream and that my mother would be around here soon. I have stayed waiting for her all this time," she finished her story.

"Do you believe any of this," Ru'ah asked Aratam.

"Of course I do. I have no reason not to," he replied. Something in the way he said that let Ru'ah know he was being sincere.

Ru'ah smiled wider than she could ever remember smiling before. She thought back to Yri and Gand's reactions to her when she told them about her mother. They were both convinced she was wrong, but now here was a stranger who did believer her. It made her believe more herself.

The two stayed up talking late into the night. Aratam made Ru'ah feel so comfortable, though she did not know exactly why. She wanted to tell him everything about her life and wanted to hear everything about his life. They related so well to one another. They both were raised as slaves living in the same household as their masters. While Ru'ah had never known her parents, Aratam did but they had both died when he was a young boy.

They talked about their friends as well. Ru'ah told him more about Yri, Beng, and Gand. She left out the parts with Gand becoming more interested in her. For some reason she just didn't want to bring that up with Aratam. She was intrigued by what he liked to do with his friends when he had a rare moment of free time. Life in the Kingdom of Enst was rather different from life in Negev. For one, life there did not revolve around the temple rituals. Instead, it revolved around keeping the palace and the royal family safe and happy. The more she learned about Aratam the more she wanted to know. He must have felt the same because he continued to ask her questions about her life. Out here in the middle of a crop field, in the middle of the desert, she had found a true friend.

The two fell asleep under the stars and slept well into the morning. When Ru'ah awoke, she had to remind herself why she was outside instead of in her hut. When she remembered Aratam, she looked around for him, but he was not there.

"Aratam?" she called out.

She heard the crops shaking as if someone was walking through them. Sure enough, Aratam emerged from the dense crop in front of her.

"Good morning," he said. "Would you like something to eat?" He gestured behind her where a pile of fruit lay enticingly.

"I've been up for a while now. I was trying to wait for you, but the more you slept the more curious I became so I decided to explore a little," Aratam continued.

The thought of Aratam wandering alone in her crop field made Ru'ah a little uneasy, but she decided not to say anything about it yet. Maybe after morning meal.

The two sat down together and once again ate of the fruit. It was still as sweet and delicious as the first time she ate it. After she was satisfied, she started up the conversation again.

"Did you find anything of interest in my field?" Ru'ah asked.

"Your field? No, nothing of interest in your field," said Aratam. "Only more of this fascinating crop."

Silence hung in the air between the two.

"I am afraid I cannot stay and enjoy more, though. I must be on my way again," Aratam finally said.

Oh, right. Ru'ah remembered Aratam was trying to find a more direct path from Enst to Kal'i in order to bring ruin to her city, Negev and possibly the known world. She knew he was under orders but the thought of the people of the city suffering hurt her greatly.

"Surly there is a way to bring understanding to the prince," she begged Aratam.

"My master is set in his ways. His mission was to see the Great Fire, and since that failed, he is determined to bring ruin to those in his way," Aratam said. "My friend, if there was another way I would try, but I fear there is nothing I can do."

My friend, he said. So, Aratam felt the same way about her after all. She was thrilled to have a true friend out here and was not ready to part with him. More importantly, she had to think of a way to stop his mission. After spending all this time out here in the desert, she felt she could do anything, but now she once again did not know what to do.

She thought back to the urgency in the priests' voices as they told her about her mission for the wick water. Perhaps this was the very thing they feared happening. If only they had fully prepared her for this mission. She thought about her long walk in the desert before the crop field came to her. There was no way she would have to make it to the wick water and back anyway. She would have failed regardless of the crop. Is that why the crop showed up when it did?

Was she supposed to only stop for a while and leave? But her mother still hadn't shown up. Was this her fault? Had she misunderstood?

All of these thoughts were swarming her mind when she remembered a time not so long ago and yet very recently, when she herself was before the Great Fire. She remembered how awed she felt in its presence. She remembered its warmth and its history with humanity. It's no wonder the prince wanted to see it so badly, it is truly amazing.

Absentmindedly, Ru'ah said, "I have seen the Great Fire."

"What did you say?" Aratam asked; his voice full of curiosity and disbelief.

"Oh, I just said I have seen the Great Fire. The priests showed it to me when I came of age," she said. She knew she probably shouldn't have said that to Aratam. She was bound to secrecy about the truth of the Great Fire and shouldn't have told anyone, but she truly felt like she could trust him with anything.

"Ru'ah you might have just solved this problem for us!" Aratam exclaimed.

"What do you mean?" Ru'ah replied.

"You have seen the Great Fire! The prince wants to see it. If you come with me back to the Kingdom of Enst, you can tell the prince about the Great Fire and perhaps then he will be satisfied!" Aratam almost shouted.

Ru'ah was so excited at the prospect of traveling to the Kingdom of Enst with Aratam. She had been alone for so long and being around him reminded her of how fulfilling it was to be around other people. Moreover, she would be able to see this kingdom that she heard so much about. Maybe she would even be able to meet some of Aratam's friends, of which he spoke so highly.

But wait, she thought, leaving with Aratam meant leaving this crop field. She had been waiting for her mother, what if her mother showed up while she was away? Could she risk that? And what would happen to the crop field if she was not here? It showed up for her, would it disappear without her? And there was her original mission to get the wick water. Should she continue that instead?

"I'm not sure that I can leave," Ru'ah said.

"But it's the only other way, besides me leaving to find another path. I thought you didn't want that," said Aratam.

"No, I don't want that, but I can't leave this crop field, I can't leave my mother!" Ru'ah cried.

"Oh, your mother, of course," Aratam sympathized.

What else could be said? They seemed at an impasse.

"Would the prince come here to me?" Ru'ah finally asked.

"No, the prince is not in the habit of being summoned," said Aratam. "And I fear what would happen to me if I came back empty handed."

Ru'ah did not want to be the cause of harm coming to Aratam, but she was still conflicted about what to do.

"Can I have some time to think about it?" she asked.

"Some time, yes, but decisions must be made soon I'm afraid," Aratam said looking up at the late positioning of the sun.

Ru'ah nodded and wandered off into the crop field. She did not want any harm to come to the people of Negev, including the Chief Priests. She did not want any harm to come to her new friend Aratam. She did not want the Great Fire to become angry and destroy everything. She did not want to leave and miss out on finding her mother. What was she to do?

She didn't know how long she walked out into the field before she sat down. Not knowing what else she could do, she posed her impossible question to the crops themselves.

"What is the right course of action?" Ru'ah said aloud.

Nothing but the rustling of leaves answered her. She stared up at the sky and posed the question again to no one in particular.

"What is the right course of action?"

Again, only silence.

Ru'ah was almost at the verge of tears when the wind started to pick up. Just like before it circled around and around. Dust flew all over her and she lay down for cover. Once again, as suddenly as it had started the wind died back down.

Ru'ah heard a voice, not aloud, but a voice within her own head.

"Whatever you choose will be the right choice," the voice within her said.

"Whatever I choose?" Ru'ah said back to the voice. Could it be that there were no right or wrong answers to this impossible question? Could it be that she was in charge of what the future would hold? That seemed like a burden too great to bear. Whatever she chose would be the right choice, so what should she choose? Staying here and waiting longer, continuing her mission to find the wick water, or going with Aratam to meet with the prince?

Ru'ah was still undecided but felt a sense of comfort knowing that she couldn't make a wrong choice. With that new knowledge, she found her way back to Aratam.

When she arrived, he had already repacked his pack and was ready to leave. She hadn't known what she was going to say to him but as soon as she looked up into his eyes, she knew what her answer would be.

"Yes, I will go with you to speak to the prince," she said.

Aratam smiles stretched across his face. "I am glad to hear that! But first, let's find you clothes that are not made of leaves."

Chapter Five

Ru'ah looked down at her clothes. She had forgotten that she had traded her traveling clothes for ones made from the crop leaves. They had become so natural on her, almost like a second skin. However, she agreed that walking into the Kingdom of Enst wearing them may cause more of a disruption than she would like.

"Yes, I suppose I should change back into my traveling clothes," Ru'ah said to Aratam. "It wouldn't do for you to be seen with a desert flower," she added with a wink.

Aratam just laughed. "I would be honored to be seen with a desert flower, but I would not want the first impression the prince has of you to be anything other than the great acolyte that you are."

Ru'ah felt her face turning red. She didn't know what she was surprised more of, that Aratam thought of her as a great acolyte or that she was thrilled that he would want to be seen with her, even as a desert flower. What were these new feelings? She had enjoyed flirting with Gand, but this was something completely different. She would have to think more on that later, for now she needed to hurry to change.

Entering her hut, Ru'ah looked over to the corner where her old clothes were stored. How long had they been there? She couldn't remember, time had become irrelevant out here in her field. It had certainly been long enough for them to look foreign. She held them up to her body. The cloth was a soft, warm material, but they were so heavy to her now.

Ru'ah slowly and carefully removed her hand made clothes, the ones she spent hours creating. And because they felt like a second skin, they were almost painful to remove. She felt somehow more exposed, more vulnerable than ever before. Outside the hut, she could hear Aratam shifting his weight. He was becoming antsy. She had to hurry. But she had to convince herself that these old clothes were safe to wear.

Slowly, carefully, she slipped her tunic over her head and shoulders. It felt chunky and unnatural over her body. It fit differently too. She could tell her body had changed since the last time she had worn it. Her arms were thicker, her shoulders wider, and her torso more filled out. After she had come to terms with her tunic, it was time to put on her hood. She remembered how excited she was when Gand showed her the proper way to wear it, but now she felt hidden, as if it took up more space than she was willing to let it.

Ru'ah took a deep breath. She knew Aratam was right, that she should wear these clothes instead of her desert ones, but she couldn't help but feel something was wrong.

"The sun is getting high in the sky," called Aratam.

He was ready to go. She could not hold him up any longer. Without any further thought, Ru'ah grabbed her woven clothes and shoved them into her bag. She then uncovered her stash of fruit and lifted several handfuls into her bag as well. She knew Aratam was well prepared for the journey back, but she wanted to have her own supplies, too.

After another deep breath, she came out of the hut.

"I am ready for our journey now," she smiled up at Aratam.

He smiled down at her, pleased that she was coming with him.

"Let the journey begin," he said.

The two walked through the crop and out into the desert sun. Ru'ah had to stop for a minute to take it all in. She had been out here just the day before but had been so distracted by Aratam that she hadn't felt the change she felt now. She couldn't put her finger on it, but something was different.

The sun blazed above her. She looked and saw only sand, white hot and blazing, for miles and miles. She missed the comfort of the field and longed for the cool shade it provided in the day, and shelter at night. How would she ever survive this trip out in the open? She was just about to tell Aratam she couldn't go when he reached for her hand.

"Not to worry, the journey is not long," Aratam said these words of comfort in a whisper.

Ru'ah was still full of doubt and fear, but somehow, she knew with Aratam, she would be able to make it to the Kingdom of Enst. And so, they set off.

On and on they walked. At first, they tried to fill the silence, but soon found comfort simply in each other's presence. Before she knew it, the sun was starting to fall to her left. She thought about her original journey. What would the priests do if they knew she was on her way to Enst instead of on her way back with the wick water? She hoped this journey was worth the cost.

Ru'ah noticed that Aratam had started to slow his pace.

"Is everything alright?" She asked.

"Yes, just looked around for a good place to set up camp," he replied.

She had hoped they would be arriving in Enst before nightfall but that clearly wasn't the case.

"How much longer will the journey be?" she asked as Aratam found the right spot.

"If we rise early enough, we should enter the gates by midday tomorrow," he said.

"Then let us rise early enough," Ru'ah replied.

Ru'ah sat down and realized how tired she was. She rummaged through her pack for some fruit to eat. She was worried that it had not kept well since leaving the field, but to her surprise, it was just as delicious as ever. After she took a few bites, herself she offered some to Aratam.

"Not to worry, I brought my own!" he said showing her that his bag was also filled to the brim with the sweet fruit.

They both laughed at this. Ru'ah was surprised again at her reaction. When she had first met Aratam, only the day before, she was possessive of her fruit and hesitant to share with him. Now she was glad he felt like he could use what he needed. After all, she thought, there's certainly enough fruit to go around.

The two lay down next to one another for warmth. As they both looked up at the stars, Ru'ah thought of something she was too afraid to ask of Aratam. Soon her curiosity got the better of her.

"Aratam," she whispered to see if he was still awake.

"Yes, Ru'ah," came the reply.

"Where do you think your parents are?" she asked so quietly she was afraid he hadn't heard her.

"They're dead," Aratam said, almost as quietly.

"Yes, I know, but where do you think they are now?" Ru'ah said stronger.

Aratam was quiet for a long time. Ru'ah was afraid she had offended him. She hadn't meant to. She didn't really even know where the question came from. The priests never said anything about what happens after someone dies, but ever since she saw her own mother, she couldn't help but wonder. She had thought her mother was dead too, maybe her mother was dead but had come back.

Aratam broke into her thoughts. "Maybe they are up there," he said pointing to the stars. "Maybe they are shining brightly down on us right now."

"I think you might be right," Ru'ah said as she gazed back up at the stars.

Ru'ah once again fell asleep thinking of what her mother said to her, "I can count the stars."

The next morning Ru'ah awoke to the sand scratching into her back. She looked over to see Aratam still asleep. The sun was just beginning its ascent. I do hope it's early enough to start our journey, she thought to herself.

Sitting up and stretching eased the pain in her back. How dearly she missed her sheltering field now.

"Aratam," she whispered. But he did not stir.

"Aratam," she said again, this time shaking him ever so slightly. She was surprised at how well he was able to sleep.

"Aratam," she said once more accompanied by a shove.

Jolting up, Aratam swung his arms in defense of himself. Ru'ah ducked just in time to avoid the blow, telling herself to never do that again.

"Ok, I'm awake now," Aratam declared.

"I see you don't enjoy being awoken," Ru'ah said.

"I was having the most intense dream," replied Aratam, "but now I can't seem to remember what it was."

Ru'ah was familiar with that sensation and was grateful she could still remember every detail of the dream where she met her mother.

"Regardless, it's time for breakfast and then our journey continues," Ru'ah said, taking command of the situation. She was the one was who was getting antsy now.

Aratam stood and shook the rest of the sleep off him. "Well, I see someone is ready to go," he joked. "I suppose there's no time for delay, let's go."

After a handful of fruit for breakfast, they were off once more.

For the first part of the morning, there was once again nothing but sand. Soon, however, Ru'ah could see the tops of buildings out in the distance.

"Ru'ah you are seeing the first signs of the great Kingdom of Enst. Welcome!" Aratam said as they walked closer.

Ru'ah was stunned. Even from far away she could tell this kingdom was vastly different from the temple city where she had grown up.

Bright reds and oranges covered the walls. Tall peaks of the palace dotted the skies. This was a kingdom that knew its own power. Ru'ah had to stop for a moment to take it all in.

"Not to worry, you're with Aratam, of the prince's House they will have to welcome you as they welcome me."

That did little to help Ru'ah. Aratam may be of the prince's household, but she knew if her mission went sour, they would both be cast out, or worse.

Ru'ah gathered the strength within herself to keep walking towards the temple. She thought back to why she started this journey in the first place. She thought of Yri and Beng. She thought of being able to return to the crop knowing she did what she could to save her people.

She kept walking until she could smell the aromas coming from within the walls. She kept walking until she could hear the shouts of haggling in the marketplace. She kept walking until she could feel the desert heat give way to the shade of the kingdom. She had arrived at this great Kingdom of Enst in the North she had heard so much about. Now it was time to meet this prince.

As Ru'ah followed Aratam through the city gates, she noticed his pace slow down until he came to a complete stop right before the entrance. She followed suit, waiting to see what he would do next.

"I need to warn you about something," Aratam said turning to face her. Her stomach knotted. What was it that made him look so fearful?

"The prince is a benevolent but strict ruler. We know he will take care of us if we stay inside the lines," Aratam explained. "The prince does not look kindly on idle chatter, especially when his enslaved workers are supposed to be serving him. I tell you this so you will not be surprised when I do not make eye contact or speak to the other enslaved workers. I advise you to do the same. Walk close to me, keep your eyes straight ahead and do not speak unless spoken to, especially to the prince."

Ru'ah was taken aback by so much formality. The priests had high expectations for their enslaved workers, but they were at least allowed their own space during the workday. This was a jarring experience for her. She nodded to let Aratam know she would follow his instructions.

With that, the two approached the guards at the gate.

"Who is it that approaches the great Kingdom of Enst," asked a guard, towering over Aratam. Ru'ah was amazed at the intricate details she saw all around her. The guard's uniforms displayed the same insignia she saw on Aratam, yet while Aratam's insignia was a bull bronze color, the guards were colored bright red and blazed in the sun. The wall that surrounded the kingdom was higher than the one surrounding Negev, with spikes looming across the top. If the purpose was to intimidate, then Ru'ah felt it was doing its job.

"Aratam of the house of the prince of the Kingdom of Enst and Ru'ah, acolyte of the Chief Priests of Negev," Aratam proclaimed to the guard.

"And what is your purpose for approaching the great Kingdom of Enst?" the guard replied.

"To return to the prince of the Kingdom of Enst after completing the mission I was sent on. I also bring the acolyte of the Chief Priests of Negev to speak to the prince as well," Aratam said.

"Very well, you and the acolyte may enter. Go straight to the palace, the prince will acknowledge you when he is ready."

Ru'ah was relieved that the exchange with the guard was over. But she was now even more frightened to see what the prince was like.

"The guards here are so serious about their business," Ru'ah whispered to Aratam as they made their way to the palace.

"Of course they are; everyone is serious about their business here. But don't let Ryn fool you, he's really a kind soul," Aratam assured Ru'ah.

Ru'ah had to stifle a laugh. "So, it's all an act?" she asked.

Aratam just shrugged and kept walking.

Ru'ah immediately felt less intimidated. When she first met Aratam he acted the same way as the guard had, but the more she came to know him, the more she realized he was a kind, kindred soul. If both Aratam and the guard could act so tough, then maybe she should take every first impression of the people of Enst as an act. Perhaps they were all kind souls that put on a tough exterior to satisfy their prince. With this new point of view, Ru'ah walked through the Kingdom of Enst with her head held high. She would not be intimidated by any of their acts, not even the prince's.

As the two approached the palace, Ru'ah was breathless. It was the most beautiful building she had ever seen. The temple of Negev was a magnificent sight, but even it dulled in comparison to this monument to opulence. The walls were a deep golden color. They may have even been made out of gold. The stairs were not as tall of the grand stair of the temple, but they were much broader and wider. Climbing them would be like climbing a mountain. However, Ru'ah felt her new strength emerge as she took one stair at a time. She was afraid she would lose her breath again, but she never did.

The doors to the palace were the same red as the guard's insignia. Surrounding the door were even more guards but with the same dull bronze insignia that Aratam wore. Ru'ah supposed the jobs were color coordinated.

"Who approaches the palace of the prince of the Kingdom of Enst?" another guard asked.

"Aratam of the house of the prince of the Kingdom of Enst and Ru'ah, acolyte of the Chief Priests of Negev," Aratam said once more.

"Yes, we have been waiting for your arrival," the new guard said. "You will wait for the prince here."

Ru'ah saw Aratam's eyebrows furrow.

"Is there a problem?" She whispered.

"Those who wish to see the prince are usually asked the wait inside the palace. I don't know why we have been asked to remain out here," Aratam explained. After a beat he added, "I'm sure it's fine."

Ru'ah was not as convinced. She was sure the change in decorum was due to her unexpected appearance. She didn't have long to deliberate because at that moment the doors swung open, and another guard ushered them into the prince's chambers.

Even greater opulence met Ru'ah's eyes. So much opulence that she could no longer take it seriously. It was as if the prince was playing his cards right out, shouting this is who I am, fear me. Ru'ah was not afraid. It was, after all, an act. Not wanting to put Aratam in any danger, she followed behind him and kept her mouth shut. She also followed suit when Aratam bowed before the enormous throne where the prince was perched.

"Aratam, I am not sure whether to be excited or disappointed that you are back so soon from your mission," the prince started. "Tell me that you have found a more direct path to the Kingdom of Kal'i in the south." Ru'ah couldn't help but hear the harsh tone the prince's voice.

Aratam stood to his full height, but since the room was so large it did not do much to change his appearance. "My Prince, I come to beg forgiveness, for I did not find this more direct path you clearly demanded."

Before Aratam could utter another word, the prince rose to his full height, "You dare return without a completed mission?" the prince said in almost a scream.

"I beg your forgiveness, I did not complete the mission, but I did bring someone who may be able to explain why," Aratam said hurriedly.

"Ah, yes, this acolyte of the Chief Priests has joined you. I cannot deny I was surprised when I heard this," the prince said. "For your sake, I hope her answers are more satisfactory."

With a wave of his hand, the prince ordered some guards to remove Aratam from the throne room. Ru'ah was amazed that Aratam went with the guards without a fight. Had he been expecting this reaction from the prince?

Alone with the prince, Ru'ah waited to be called upon. She was about to lose patience and speak out of turn when the prince finally acknowledged her.

"Acolyte, why are you here?" the prince demanded.

"I am here at behalf of my people of the temple city Negev." Ru'ah replied.

"What of them?" the prince asked.

Ru'ah took a deep breath and began her tale.

"When my priests heard that you had forbidden your people from coming to the Great Fire, I was sent into the desert to find wick water in order to appease the Great Fire. We know the power it has and its ability to destroy when it is unsatisfied. As I journeyed through the desert, I was delayed on my mission for the wick water. That is when I met your enslaved worker, Aratam. Aratam told me that he was looking for a more direct path between your Kingdom Enst in the North and the Kingdom of Kal'i in the south. This path would cut off the temple city completely and surely destroy my people. I come to beg you to reconsider."

"Aratam knows that I do not oblige to begging, surely this cannot be serious," the prince said, as a reedy edge crept into his rising voice. Ru'ah took note that he sounded more like a petulant child than a ruler of a great kingdom. "Why are you here?" the prince asked, fully screaming now.

"I am here because I have seen the Great Fire," Ru'ah continued. At that the prince stopped in his tracks.

"You?" the prince's voice dropped suddenly, but kept the nasally whine, "You have seen the Great Fire. I have been denied, but you, you who are a mere acolyte, have seen the Great Fire," the prince complained.

"I was surprised myself when the priests allowed me into its presence. And I did not see it until I came of age, a time not too long ago. I am risking my life, but I have come here to tell you about the Great Fire in hopes that you will spare my people."

"You gamble that I will trade my right to see the Great Fire for a mere tale?" The whine had left the prince's voice, replaced with the haughty displeasure he had when they first arrived.

"I offer you what I have in hopes that it will be enough. The priests will never let you into the temple, not while there is still breath in their bodies. This is the only other way to have knowledge of the Great Fire," Ru'ah pleaded.

Ru'ah braced herself for the prince's outrage. Now that she had been in his presence, she knew he would not likely take this second-rate option. She said a silent prayer to the Great Fire that this would work, that the prince would spare her people. She chanced a look at the prince to get a clue as to how he would respond. To her surprise, he appeared deep in thought.

"My parents are ill," the prince finally said; all traces of pomp or whine absent.

"Is that why you rule?" Ru'ah asked.

"Yes, they are both ill. They have been getting sicker and sicker for months now. I have been giving generously to the Great Fire but to no avail. I wanted to see it myself, to demand answers and action. Why were my parents suffering? Why did the Great Fire not intervene on their behalf? I need to see the Great Fire, to save my parents."

Surprised by this sudden change in vulnerability, Ru'ah dared approach the throne.

"My parents are dead, too," Ru'ah shared. "Or at least I thought they were."

Ru'ah placed her hand on the prince's arm while he started to cry. It was all an act. Of course it was all an act; he is not a petulant child; he is a hurting child. She knew the pain he felt at the thought of losing his parents. He was older than she was, by a few years, yet he still was heartbroken at this loss. He was the ruler of a great kingdom, the master to many enslaved workers. And yet, he felt the same pain and suffering at the loss of family as anyone else.

Ru'ah thought back to her life as the temple acolyte. However long ago that was. At the time, she longed for a different life, a life that was not so routine. Yet now she longed to go back, it was such a simpler time. She knew what she was doing. She knew what her days were going to be like. But now, things where too different. Each day had a new challenge, a new twist. She would never have expected to be in the presence of this prince, let alone comfort him while he cried. She would never have expected to meet someone who was enslaved by this prince, let alone befriend them.

No, she thought. Life in the temple city was easier and simpler, but she would not go back. She was her own person now and was on her own adventure. She would never have expected to be here, but here she was, advocating for her people. This is where she wanted to be.

Ru'ah knelt next to the prince as he dried his eyes. She did not know what would happen next, but she was not afraid.

"I wish to see the Great Fire, but I will first hear your tale then make my decision," the prince announced.

Ru'ah stood back up, cleared her throat, and began to tell the tale of the Great Fire as she remembered Yawen told her.

"The Great Fire was and is and shall be. At the beginning of time, the Great Fire created the desert sand. From that sand came people, and from those people came kingdoms. But the Great Fire ruled at will. The Great Fire gave the people warmth and comfort, but the Great Fire also destroyed. The people lived and died by its will.

There were two people – a united couple who first learned to work with the Great Fire. They discovered that if they provided sacrifice to it, it would stay in one place. If they kept it sated, it kept them warm and alive. Soon all people came to pay homage to the Great Fire. They would bring the Great Fire meat and it would make the meat delicious. People could bring the Great Fire into their homes and as long as it was sated, it would keep them warm and not destroy their homes.

As the united priests grew older, they realized they could not keep up with such a large fire. They decided to bring a small part of the Great Fire inside of a temple to better keep up with it. They continued to offer praise and bring homage to the Great Fire inside the temple. They passed on this story to the next Chief Priests who then passed it on to the next. This story was passed down to me as the acolyte. And I myself saw the very same fire that those first Chief Priests brought into the temple all those years ago."

Ru'ah stopped to catch her breath. Even recalling the vision of the Great Fire took so much of her energy. She looked at the prince and could tell him was enraptured with the story as well.

"Describe to me this Great Fire," the prince insisted.

"It is the most beautiful sight I have ever seen. Its flame is small, but it is enough to light a whole room. The flame dances in a shade of blue that is deeper than the sky at twilight. The power emanating off this flame brought me to my knees. I was moved to tears by its very presence. I can understand why only priests are entrusted with its image. I believe the world would lose itself if it knew the true beauty of this flame."

"Ru'ah I beg you to stop," the prince whispered. "Your description is making me long to see it even more, yet I fear what I would do if I did see it."

Ru'ah knew exactly what the prince meant. She had not considered the power of the Great Fire until she had to describe it for herself. She remembered a time when she thought the rituals were unnecessary but now that she had seen it for herself, she would never question them again. She could only hope the prince would realize the danger he would be putting everyone in if he did not change his mind.

Ru'ah dared ask the question, "Have I satisfied your curiosity enough to convince you to stop your mission?"

These words snapped the prince out of his reverence. "No. I still demand answers from this Great Fire. Why has it brought this tragedy upon my life?" the prince said.

Ru'ah tried to hide her disappointment. She was at a loss, if the prince was this convinced that he needed to exact revenge, then she didn't know what else she could do.

"I beg of you not to bring any more tragedy to this world. I fear that is what would happen if you angered the Great Fire," she begged.

But the prince had put is act back on. The vulnerability Ru'ah knew was there hid once again.

"I shall do what I must until I am satisfied with an answer," the prince declared.

"But consider the suffering of others, consider my suffering. I too thought I lost my parents, I understand your pain, but I fear your mission is misguided," Ru'ah cried.

"You said that before, you thought you lost your parents, what does that mean?" the prince asked, a hint of his vulnerability showing through.

Without hesitation, Ru'ah explained the rest of her story. "I have never met my parents. I have always known them to be dead. I was raised by the Chief Priests in Negev. Yet the night before I left the temple city, I had a dream when I was surrounded by a crop field. In the crop field there was someone else. When I asked who she was, she told me she was who I needed her to be. I knew it was my mother in that field. And I knew this was more than a dream. My mother was calling for me, waiting for me to come find her.

The next day I awoke to hear the news that the priests were sending me on a journey. I knew that during the journey I would find my mother. I walked and walked in the desert for days hoping to find this field, but it never appeared. Many times, I heard my mother calling me. Finally, the day came when I could walk no more. I lay down for the last time and cried. I planned to cry myself into the end. But when I woke from my tears, I found what I had been looking for. I was in the middle of the crop at last.

I knew my mother would be there, somewhere, so I looked. I stayed in the crop field many days waiting and waiting, when Aratam arrived by chance. I am eager to return to this crop field in hopes that by then my mother will be there waiting for me."

Ru'ah could tell the prince was stunned. He looked at her with fear or confusion, she couldn't quite tell.

"So, this field just appeared?" the prince finally asked.

"Yes," Ru'ah replied. "I believe it found me in the desert."

"I do not understand, how can a field of crop just pop up in the middle of the desert. I am a learned man; I know how long it takes between sowing and harvesting. Crops need proper soil and water and care. They don't just pop up, and certainly not in the middle of a desert."

"If I had not been there myself, I would not have believed it either, but I swear it is true. Aratam has seen it as well."

The prince looked toward the door that the guards took Aratam through. Ru'ah thought for a moment he was going to have Aratam come back, but instead the prince paced before his throne.

"No, I cannot believe it," he muttered, over and over again. "How do you know it was your mother?" the prince asked, suddenly switching his focus.

"I … I just knew," Ru'ah replied. How could she explain this to the prince? She just knew it was her mother. She felt a connection unlike any other she had ever felt before. Who else could it have been?

The prince considered her answer for a moment then kept pacing.

Again, he stopped to ask, "How do you know it was more than a dream?"

Ru'ah was at a loss. The questions the prince was asking were fair questions, but she didn't think he would be satisfied with her answers. She knew because she knew. That's all there was too it.

This time the prince did not wait for her to answer before he started pacing and muttering again.

Ru'ah started to become afraid. She knew the prince had a vulnerability and was putting on an act, but he still had the power to throw her out of his kingdom. He still had the power to destroy the temple city of Negev and possibly even the known world. She had to think fast of something to do to convince him she told the truth.

"I can prove it," she finally said.

The prince kept walking so she called louder, "I can prove it."

"Prove it? You are going to take me out to the desert to wonder around for a crop field that may not exist. I will not be made such a fool," the prince sneered.

Ru'ah shook off the insult. "No, there is no need to even leave this room. I can prove it here."

The prince looked long and hard at her. She could not be sure what he was thinking, but prayed his vulnerability would come back.

"How? How can you prove it?" the prince demanded.

"I will prove it. I can show you the fruit of the harvest without leaving this chamber."

This got the prince's attention. "You have the fruit with you, here? I must see it."

"I will gladly show it to you, but first I need Aratam to be returned to this room," Ru'ah said.

"You are in no position to demand such a thing," the prince replied.

"I am not making idle demands," Ru'ah explained. "The fruit is in his bag, and since he has also tasted of it, he can share the wonders of it with you as well. Aratam is your faithful servant; he would not lead you astray."

The prince looked again at the door, pondering. "Yes, I suppose that will do," he said.

He rapped his fist on his throne and immediately the guards returned to his presence.

"Bring my servant Aratam to my presence at once," the prince called to the guards.

After some hustle and bustle, Aratam was returned and the guards once more left.

"Aratam, I hear you can share with me the secrets of this crop," the prince said.

Aratam looked over at Ru'ah. She nodded to assure him this was not a trap.

"I do not know that I can share its secrets, but I can tell you what I know," Aratam replied.

"Then tell me," the prince said.

"When I found Ru'ah in the desert she was surrounded by a field of the strangest fruit. After she was assured I meant her no harm, she invited me into the field and fed me this fruit. It was unlike anything I have ever tasted before. It was sweet and satisfying. I no longer hungered or thirsted after eating it."

"And you have brought some of this fruit with you?" the prince asked.

"Yes, my prince. It sustained us on the journey back. We needed nothing else, no other food or water. Just this fruit was enough for us to survive on," Aratam said.

"Ru'ah tells me you have some with you right now. That is why you have been called back, to share it with me," said the prince.

"Yes, prince I have an offering of it for you. I am pleased to share it," said Aratam.

Aratam took the pack off his back and untied the strap. Ru'ah could see that it was still full of the fruit. It was still a radiant purple color and still smelled as fresh as the day it was grown. Aratam gathered a piece of fruit and brought it before the prince.

The prince was just about to taste of it when he stopped. "No, I will not be the first to taste of this in my throne room. Aratam you would give your life for me, I know that, so I will have you taste of it first."

Ru'ah could see the hurt in Aratam's eyes. The prince surely didn't think that Aratam would give anything poisoned to him.

But Aratam did as he was told. The prince watched with bated breath as Aratam took a bite of the wondrous fruit. Ru'ah would have been happy to join in the feast, but she dared not move, for Aratam's sake.

Finally, the prince was satisfied that the offering was, indeed, not poisoned.

He took a piece out of Aratam's hand and held it up to his lips. Ru'ah watched as the prince took a bite, slowly chewed, and swallowed. Aratam chanced a glance back at her. He looked just as tense as she felt.

Ru'ah looked back at the prince and saw tears flowing from his eyes.

"This truly is magical," the prince whispered. "I admit I doubted you, Ru'ah, but your story is true. I know your entire story is true now. How could anyone who brings this sweet fruit to me tell anything but the truth?"

Aratam and Ru'ah exhaled. The prince was finally sated.

"Do you trust me when I say you mustn't anger the Great Fire?" Ru'ah asked of the prince.

"Great Fire?" sputtering, the prince turned an incredulous look toward Ru'ah, "I have no need of the Great Fire! It is this crop that I now must have."

Chapter Six

Ru'ah froze. She did not know what the prince had in mind, but she had a feeling it would not be to her benefit.

Like a flash, the prince ran to Aratam, grabbed his bag right out of his hands, and rushed out of a back door from the throne room.

Without even looking at Aratam, Ru'ah ran after the prince. Where was he going with this bag of her crop? Ru'ah found that she was running after the prince through a long and narrow corridor. It was as ornate as the rest of the palace and guards lined the walls who looked just as surprised to see the prince running through the halls as she was. Ru'ah felt someone running right behind her. She thought it was one of the guards but looked back to see it was Aratam.

"What is going on?" She yelled to him.

"I'm not sure. Maybe the prince has gone mad," Aratam called back.

They had both forgotten they were still within earshot of the prince. He shouted back to both of them, "I am not mad, I am alive, and soon my parents will be as well." Right then it occurred to Ru'ah what was happening. The prince was taking this miracle fruit to his parents.

Ru'ah ran faster to catch up with the prince. If he had told her what he wants she would have gladly shared. She was just about to reach him when he stopped in front of a heavily guarded door.

"Prince, allow us to come with you," Ru'ah offered as the guards made way for the prince to enter.

He looked back and considered them for a moment.

"My parents have been ill for many months now. They have withered away to practically nothing. They are in constant pain. Though they try to hide it from me, I know they are suffering. If anything can help them, it is this miracle fruit."

"Yes, I think you are right Prince. This fruit saved me as well. I ask that I can be in the presence of another miracle. To see the parents you love so much," Ru'ah pleaded.

'Very well. You who know the miracle of the fruit may be in the presence of the great King and Queen of the Kingdom of Enst," the prince replied and opened the door to another world.

As lavish as the rest of the palace was, this room was modest at best. The dull light of individual candles lit the sides of the room. There were no windows, just plain walls and a low ceiling. Ru'ah noticed it was warmer in this room than it had been in the rest of the palace. There was also a strong aroma coming from the other end of the room. It smelled of sweet flowers and fresh bread. She loved those smells on their own, but in this room, they seemed to be masking something else, something foul.

The room was a modest size, big enough to fit two beds and still have room for several people to move around comfortably. Ru'ah intuitively felt like she needed to make as little noise as possible when in there. She could hear labored breathing coming from the beds and did not want to disturb whoever were the occupants.

She noticed the prince hesitate as well. She sensed fear come over him, as if he did not want to be in this reality. In this room, his mask was truly uncovered. In this room, he was not a prince who commanded a kingdom, but a scared little boy who wanted his parents to comfort him.

Ru'ah took the prince by the hand. He looked over at her. She could see any mistrust clear from his eyes when he looked into hers. She knew he felt the same connection she felt. The connection of loss and fear, the connection of wanting things to be different. Aratam joined in this moment. Ru'ah remembered that he too knew the sting of losing people he loved the most.

Together the three approached the beds. Ru'ah could see the faces of nobility through the scarring of months of sickness.

The King looked up at his son and tears filled his deep, beautiful eyes. "My son," the king said, in a hoarse whisper. "You are here now, or is this just a dream?"

"It is no dream, father," the prince replied. "I am here, and I have help."

The king reached over to his queen to get her attention. She, too, looked up at her son.

"He has come to us, my queen," the king said in a labored breath.

"My son, my prince, you are so kind to come to us even now," the queen murmured.

Ru'ah looked once more at the prince. It was no wonder he wore a mask. How could he face the day knowing his parents were withering away right behind these walls? Ru'ah had never known her parents and still missed them deeply. She couldn't imagine the pain of going through this, of watching her parents die. No wonder this crop was so important to this prince.

"Mother, Father, I am here to save you. I have brought a miracle," the prince said through tears.

"Oh, my dear you are kind to say that" the queen said.

Ru'ah couldn't tell if the queen was simply too sick to realize what the prince had said, or if the queen didn't believe what the prince had said.

But the prince was determined to show his parents this fruit. He reached into the bag and pulled out a ripe purple pod. The fruit was radiant enough to fill the room. Even the queen and king's eyes could not look away from it.

"Mother, Father, this is a miraculous fruit. You must eat of it. I did, and I immediately felt as if I could do anything. Like I could run all the way across the desert, like I could even fly. I know this fruit will save you from this illness. Then we can live and reign together. I will gladly give you back your throne, Father. I will gladly sit at your feet once again and learn from you. I will no longer have a reign of fear, but we can all have a reign of peace, a reign where we pay homage to this miracle crop. Please, Father, Mother won't you try some of this fruit?"

Ru'ah saw the look in their eyes. It was the same look she saw Beng give the little children when they begged for another treat. She was amazed to see that, even in this state, these parents together decided to appease their only child.

With a great feat of strength, the king and queen sat up. The prince embraced them both and began, once again, to cry. Ru'ah and Aratam made themselves small in the corner of the room. They knew enough to know this was a family affair. They were outsiders looking into this intimate moment between parents and child. Ru'ah guessed that like her, Aratam was feeling a pang of loss for his own parents.

Finally, the prince let his parents go and gave them each a piece of the fruit. The parents looked at one another and then together ate this offering from their son.

As the fruit coursed through their bodies, Ru'ah could see years melt off their faces. She knew what they were feeling. When she ate the fruit, she felt stronger than she ever had. All her hunger and thirst disappeared completely. Just like the prince had said, she felt like she could run the length of the desert. She knew the even the worst illness could not stand up to the power of the fruit. But in a moment, her thoughts were interrupted.

"Oh, my son, my son!" the king shouted out. The décor had not changed, but the room was now lighter, brighter. The king stood to his full height. The queen came over to her united partner and embraced him. They kissed as if for the first time. Then, they both embraced their son. This time, strong arms enveloped one another. The family was once again healthy and whole. So much joy filled the room that everyone, including Ru'ah and Aratam couldn't help but laugh.

It had worked; the crop had brought these two people back to life. This family could continue being a family. And Ru'ah was able to breathe a sigh of relief. This meant that the Kingdom of Enst would not break ties with the temple city of Negev. The Great Fire would not take its anger out on her people. She could go back to her crop field in peace.

As the family continued to embrace, she looked over at Aratam. She was so grateful he had shown up in the middle of the desert. She was grateful for his friendship and his willingness to help her save her people. Without him, she would never have had an audience with the prince. Just thinking about their journey together over the few short days they knew each other brought tears to her eyes.

He must have sensed her looking at him because he looked over at her. In the blink of an eye, he reached over to her and pulled her into a bear hug. She loved the way she rested in the crook of his arms. She hugged him back with all of her might.

This was a perfect day, Ru'ah thought. She could not have asked for a better miracle than a family reunited.

She looked back over at the prince. His parents had finally let him go but they were still all smiles.

All the exuberance must have started to take a toll on the king. Ru'ah thought he would need a little more fruit to regain his full strength. She watched as the king closed his eyes and took a deep breath.

He looked up at his son and said, "My son, my son. I love you."

Then, he laid back down, closed his eyes and breathed no more.

Everyone in the room: the queen, the prince, Aratam and Ru'ah stood in shock as they realized that even after eating this miracle crop, the king was dead.

Ru'ah lost the ability to hear, the ringing in her ears was overwhelming. How could this happen? She couldn't make sense of it. The king was alive, he was whole, but now he lay lifeless right before her eyes.

After a moment, she looked around and realized the ringing in her ears had given way to the sound of a heart breaking. The prince kneeled beside his father's body, inconsolable. He screamed and screamed at the top of his lungs. Throughout the screams, Ru'ah heard him wailing words like 'why' and 'no'; the same words her own heart was making.

The queen had gently placed one hand on the king's chest and one hand on her son's shoulder. She was a pillar of strength in the face of this immense grief. She made no noise but stood strong, even though Ru'ah could see the pain on her face.

Ru'ah left Aratam's side to go comfort the bereaved family. For a moment, she shared in their suffering. When she put her hand on the prince's shoulder, she felt his grief rush into her body. She could feel the heaviness in her chest as sobs begged to come out of her own eyes. She looked closer at the king. He was a handsome man, with silver hair and a look of nobility even in death. He also looked kind. She wished she had been able to meet him before this moment. Perhaps the priests had memories of him. He must have come to Negev at some point. She wanted so badly to speak to him, to know his stories. If she felt this way as someone who did not know him at all, she could not imagine how his own son felt. She squeezed the prince's shoulder out of condolence.

That was enough to shake the prince out of this moment of sheer misery. He looked up at Ru'ah and lost it.

Once again ringing filled her ears. When she came to, she heard the prince screaming again, but this time at her.

"How could you, I trusted you!" he shouted.

Ru'ah couldn't understand what was happening. She knew the prince was in deep sorrow but why was he blaming her for his father's death.

She was grateful when Aratam came to her defense when she was at a loss for words.

"It's not her fault," Aratam shouted back. "We all ate the fruit. We all felt its healing powers. You yourself did only a few moments ago. You cannot blame Ru'ah for any of this."

This did not appease the prince. Ru'ah noticed the fire in his eyes as he turned from her and screamed into the abyss.

Ru'ah braced herself for more shouting, but the prince changed tactics. He went around the room and started smashing the candles against the wall. One by one, the lights went out until the room was completely dark. This did not slow the prince down though. He simply opened the door that led back to the main palace. In a flash, he was out of sight.

Ru'ah grabbed Aratam's hand and they started running. Even though the prince had blamed her, she did not want him to cause anyone else harm, including himself.

They followed the prince through the halls and watched him smash the trinkets that had just a few moments before decorated the walls in splendor.

Ru'ah noticed the guards looking befuddled. They were supposed to protect the prince from an invasion of the palace. What were they supposed to do when it was the prince was the invader in his own palace?

The prince continued his rampage all the way back to the throne room, where Aratam and Ru'ah finally caught up with him. They tried to grab him to stop him, but he kept overpowering them. Maybe it was the grief that helped him slip through their grip. He was about to head out the door to ransack the kingdom itself when Ru'ah heard behind her the sweet sound of singing.

The prince stopped in his tracks, turned around and fell to his knees crying. His mother, the queen, kept singing a lullaby as she came to hold her son. Ru'ah figured it was the lullaby she sang to him as a young boy. Maybe his father sang it too.

The queen rocked her son as if he were a little boy again. She sang and sang until he was somewhat pacified. Ru'ah looked with relief to

Aratam. He looked like he had just as many questions as she did, but for now they both remained silent. Instinct told them both to let this mother and son have a moment alone.

Ru'ah then looked around at the guards who had filled the room noticing they looked around nervously at each other and at the prince and queen. She wanted to tell them it would be all right, that they could go back to their jobs, but she did not want to chance ruining the moment again. After a while the guards must have felt like things were calmed down enough because they did leave the throne room. Once again it was only Ru'ah, Aratam, and the prince and queen.

The queen continued to sing the lullaby, but she was getting quieter and quieter until she was singing in no more than a whisper. She hummed one more round of the song and became quiet.

The prince had stopped crying as well. Ru'ah held her breath to see what would happen next. The prince looked up at his mother and like a child trying to figure out the ways of the world, said to her, "I don't understand. The fruit was supposed to heal him, why did he die?"

Ru'ah wanted to know the answer to that as well.

The queen gestured for her and Aratam to join her and her son sitting on the floor. Ru'ah felt the warmth of her motherly presence and longed for her own mother to join in this circle.

Ru'ah had been strong for so long, she just wanted to collapse, for someone to hold her like the queen was holding her prince. She wanted someone to explain the ways of the world to her. So she graciously sat next to the queen and waited for her to make things right.

"My son, the fruit did heal your father," the queen explained.

The prince started to protest but the queen continued, "your father grew sick many years ago. He tried so hard to hide it from you, from me, from everyone. He continued to rule until you came of age. It was so important to him to show you how to be a good king. But he was so sick he was not able to do so. You were kept out of the throne room more than your father would have liked simply because he did not want to show you his pain.

When you came of age, he took a step back and allowed you to rule. For several years he told no one how sick he really was so that he could guide you. He was so proud when you would come to ask his counsel. But he got sicker and sicker. And you came to him less and less. He knew it was time for him to prepare to leave this world. He had done his job all he could."

"But he didn't die, he has been alive this whole time," the prince interrupted.

"I'm afraid that is my fault," the queen said. "Even though your father was ready to die, I was not ready for him to leave me behind. I did all I could to heal him. I brought in as many healers as I could. I sacrificed to the Great Fire as much as I could. I made myself sick trying to heal him. Finally, a few months ago I became too weak to care for myself, let alone anyone else. That is when we entered confinement. My son, you have been kind to take care of us as much as you have over these past months. You have sent healers yourself and have sacrificed, I know. And today, you finally did heal me and your father."

"No, I didn't. I didn't heal him. He is dead," the prince cried.

"My son, no one lives forever. There are those who try, but I know of no one who has succeeded. Your father was ready to die, and so he died. But you healed him today. You made a way for him to say goodbye to you as his old self, as the man he was before he became so sick. You healed him by allowing him to tell you one last time how much he loved you and by letting him see that you had become the man he hoped you would be. You may not have caused him to live longer, but you healed him so that he could die well."

The prince stood up from the floor. Ru'ah watched as he paced and pondered what his mother just said. She too needed to ponder these words. She had never considered healing in these terms. Perhaps the queen had a point. But then a thought occurred to Ru'ah.

"Why did you not die?" she asked the queen.

The queen smiled softly, "I'm afraid I was not ready to go yet. I wanted to hang on a little longer. I know that one day I will join the king, but for now I want to stay with my prince."

Ru'ah could understand the love between this mother and son. It was the same love she felt for her own mother, even though she had yet to meet her. She suddenly longed to return to the crop field but knew her work in Enst was not done yet.

She got up off the floor and approached the prince who had returned to his throne. "I must ask you now if you will drop your plan to cut off the Negev. I came here to advocate for my people. I ask you to consider my plea."

The queen joined the prince in the throne next to him. "What is this about" she asked her son.

Ru'ah saw the prince looking down at his feet, like a child who had been caught being naughty. If the situation weren't so grave, she would have laughed. Instead, she stood patiently waiting for the prince to answer his mother.

The queen must have sensed how grave the situation was as well because she dismissed both Ru'ah and Aratam. They quickly left out the door that led into the kingdom, leaving the prince to answer for what he had done.

"What a day," Aratam said once they were alone.

"I do not wish for another one like it," Ru'ah replied. "Although your kingdom is a sight!"

Ru'ah looked out before her. The sun was getting low in the sky, but it hit the kingdom in a way that made it light up. The colors of the buildings sparkled. The merchants and tradespeople glowed as they moved about. Ru'ah felt a tinge of remorse that she was not in her own temple city with her own people.

"Now that we are free of the prince, allow me to show you around," Aratam offered.

Ru'ah graciously accepted. She was ready to be far away from the torrent of emotions the palace held.

Together they walked around the kingdom. Aratam showed her places of importance to him, like where he and his friends would play in a back alley when he was a child, and where his parents taught him how to haggle in the market. She asked some questions now and then, but mostly she just listened. She liked the way his eyes lit up when he talked about his life. It was true that his life was not his own as an enslaved person, but he was able to find joy in it, nonetheless.

Finally, Aratam showed her his own small home that was near the palace. It was the home he once shared with his parents but since they had died, he lived alone. Small though it was it felt like a good home. It reminded Ru'ah so much of Yri and Beng's small home with all of their shared love. The two sat in silence at Aratam's table for a few moments. They were both exhausted from the day.

"May I have some privacy?" Ru'ah asked.

"Of course, I can offer you my sleeping quarters if you would like," Aratam replied.

"Yes, that will do if you do not mind," Ru'ah said as she stood.

She walked over to the only other room in the house. It was sealed off by a curtain, but it would be just enough to give her a moment alone – something she had not had since Aratam had shown up in the crop field only a few days ago.

Ru'ah felt the heaviness of her clothes once again. She had been so distracted earlier she had forgotten about them, but now they felt heavier than ever. With relief Ru'ah remembered she had packed away her crop clothing. She quickly reached into her bag to make sure they were wearable. They were just as they were when she packed them. Ru'ah slid off her traveling clothes and exchanged them for these other clothes, the ones she had made herself. She was about to put her traveling clothes back into her pack when she decided she would not need them anymore. She left them on Aratam's sleeping mat and returned to the table in the main part of his home.

"Well, you are a desert flower again," Aratam teased.

"I have no need to the clothes that belonged to my priests. I know the prince will do right by me and so I will continue to live on my own in the desert for as long as I need to in order to find my mother," Ru'ah proclaimed.

Aratam nodded his agreement. "You are free," he said.

"Freedom is a right to all," Ru'ah said. She didn't know where those words came from, but she knew they were true.

"Yes, well the prince will think otherwise," Aratam replied.

"The prince has been through a revelation today. Do you not think he would see the truth of freedom if only we were to explain it to him?" Ru'ah posed.

Aratam sat in silence for a few moments. Ru'ah couldn't understand why he was hesitating. She had found her own freedom, so could he.

"The prince is one in a long line of princes. He has known this life and this life only. It will not occur to him that this life is oppressive to so many others," Aratam said.

"We must explain it to him," Ru'ah insisted.

"I fear that would do more harm than good. The prince is not one who is used to being told what to do. The queen was able to help him see the truth of healing, but I do not think she will be on our side in this argument. She too has only known this life," Aratam replied.

"Then we must help your people find their own freedom, like I did," Ru'ah said.

"Ru'ah you are in a situation I have never heard of before. You were sent on a mission from your masters, but in that mission, you found your freedom. I cannot guarantee that for my people. If I lead them in a revolt or out to the desert and they die, what would that make me? The risk is too great," Aratam resigned.

Ru'ah felt defeated. She knew Aratam had a point but there had to be a way to freedom for all people.

She wanted to keep discussing this with him, but they were interrupted by a knock on the door.

Aratam got up to answer. It was some palace guards who came to bring them back to the throne room. The prince was demanding their audience.

Ru'ah and Aratam followed the guard back to the palace. It had only been earlier that day that Ru'ah first laid eyes on it, but now it looked smaller, less ornate. She had seen its secrets and knew what lay behind the façade.

Even so, when she came before the prince and queen in all their glory she kneeled before them.

"Arise, Ru'ah acolyte of the Chief Priests of the Great Fire. Arise Aratam loyal servant to the Kingdom of Enst," the queen commanded them.

"My son has told me your tale and why you have brough this miracle crop to this kingdom. I want to thank you for this gift, and although the king has left this life, the crop has healed this family."

Ru'ah was amazed at the queen's presence. There were no signs of her sickness. She stood tall and powerful, a true queen. Even her son paled in comparison to her.

"I have ordered the guards to prepare my king's body for a proper kingly burial. Soon, they will bring him into his throne room and the announcement will be made before the whole kingdom," the queen continued. "As we wait for that, my son will speak with you."

Ru'ah watched as the queen sat down to make way for the prince. He stood up from him throne and approached Ru'ah.

"My friend, I too wish to thank you for coming to this kingdom and bringing this crop. You came to save your people, and in the process, you saved my family. I will miss my father for the rest of my life, but I can now rule knowing that he is resting in peace. I will keep my word to not cut off the temple city."

Ru'ah was filled with joy at the prince's promise. She had completed what she came to do, now she could go back to her crop without fear. But the prince was not done speaking yet.

"My friend, I ask now for a blessing from you, the keeper of this miracle crop. I ask that you bless my reign, that it may be prosperous for my kingdom and for the whole world."

Ru'ah did not know what to do. She had seen the priests give blessings to people, but she had never considering giving a blessing to anyone herself. Who was she to give a blessing? But how could she refuse this prince? She had seen how volatile his nature could be and did not want to risk him changing his mind. Slowly, she placed her hand on his head as she had seen the priests do.

"Prince, you have my blessing as keeper of the crop. May your reign be prosperous, and may your reign be long," she said.

That must have satisfied the prince because he smiled and then embraced her. "Thank you, thank you, thank you."

At that, the prince returned to his throne and the guards brought the body of the king into the throne room.

After the king was placed in the middle of the room, the guards opened all the doors that led to the outside kingdom. Ru'ah heard a horn blow three times and watched as the citizens of the kingdom stopped what they were doing, come out of their houses and gather around the steps of the palace.

Once things had settled down a guard called out loud and clear, "The King had left this life." At that all the citizens fell to their knees. The guard continued. "The new King reigns."

Ru'ah watched as the queen and prince came before the people. The queen gathered the crown from her dead partner's head and gestures for the prince to kneel before her. She then placed the crown on his head while the kingdom cheered. He was no longer a prince; he was The King of The Kingdom of Enst.

The horn blew three more times, and the people went back to their work. The guards went back to their positions. Ru'ah was once again alone with Aratam, the queen and now king. Her mission to Enst was complete and she needed to return to her crop as soon as she could. She waited for the king and queen to return to their thrones and then kneeled before them once more.

"Arise my friend, Ru'ah," the king commanded.

"King of Enst, I am pleased to have helped heal your family, I am pleased to have given you the blessing you desire, but now I must return to my crop field," Ru'ah said.

"Ah, yes, I was afraid this would happen. Is there no way you can stay?" the king posed.

"I am afraid not, there is unfished business I must attend to," Ru'ah replied.

"Very well, I will allow you to leave my kingdom at first light," the king said.

"There is one more thing," Ru'ah continued.

"Yes?" the king asked.

"Aratam has been a friend and guide to me these past few days. He knows the desert better than I do, I ask the king grant Aratam permission to accompany me back to the crop field, if he so desires," Ru'ah asked. She chanced a glance as Aratam who looked pleased at her request.

"Aratam, is this something you desire?" the king asked.

"Yes, my king, I will gladly lead Ru'ah through the desert," Aratam said.

"Very well. I will give you seven days to return back to my kingdom," the prince commanded. "For now, I will have you sit with myself and my queen mother for evening meal," said the king.

After dinner, Ru'ah returned with Aratam to his small home. He was gracious enough to let her rest on his sleeping mat while he slept on the floor of the main room. She couldn't remember the last time she had slept on her mat back at the temple. She tossed and turned for a while, trying to get comfortable. She had grown so used to sleeping in the desert, a mat was almost too luxurious. She also found that the food she had eaten for the evening meal did not satisfy her for long. About halfway through the night, she got up to eat a piece of her fruit. She realized how much had changed in such a short amount of time since finding the crop field.

Finally, once her stomach was full, she drifted off to sleep dreaming about being back in the comfort of her crop hut.

Ru'ah was awoken by Aratam gently nudging her shoulder.

"Ru'ah, it is first light. It is time to go," he whispered.

She arose and stretched, then she was ready to go.

"I thank you for accompanying me," Ru'ah said to Aratam as they walked out of his hut.

"It is my pleasure," he said. The way he looked at her made her realize he was sincere, that he really did want to come with her all the way back out to the desert. She couldn't deny how pleased she was at this.

Together they walked through the morning without saying much. The events of yesterday were still fresh in her mind, and she needed all of her energy to keep moving. Maybe one day they would talk about what they went through that day with the prince, but not right now.

They stopped again for the evening but again didn't say much. Just being in each other's presence was enough. Ru'ah laid down that night and looked up at the stars. She hoped that her mother would be waiting for them when they returned to the field tomorrow. She thought of all the things she would say to her. She thought of how much she wanted to embrace her mother, like the prince was able to embrace his. She thought about how much easier it was to sleep out under the stars than it had been to sleep in a bed. Maybe that is what she and her mother could do – live forever out in the crop field on their own. They would be free together. Maybe even Aratam could stay with them. Ru'ah fell asleep that night thinking about how nice that life could be.

The next morning, Ru'ah awoke with the sun. This time it was she who nudged Aratam awake. But he did not seem as excited as she was to continue the journey.

"Ru'ah we need to talk," he said.

She was surprised at this since they spent most of the last day in silence, but she allowed him room to say what was on his mind.

"Once we return to the crop field, I must leave you," he said. "The king only gave me a week leave, and I must return."

Ru'ah was crushed. She had allowed herself to believe that Aratam would defy the king's command to stay with her.

"I understand. Perhaps one day soon you can return," she said, full of hope.

"Since the prince has decided not to cut off ties with the temple city, there is no need for me to travel through the desert," Aratam explained. "But maybe … you could return to Enst."

Ru'ah had not considered returning to Enst. She had so longed to be with her mother, she did not want to give up on that dream. Aratam must have read what she was thinking because he said, "it's not something you have to decide right now."

Ru'ah did not want to be apart from Aratam. She didn't know what do to. For now, all she could do was keep walking. And so, she did. The rest of the morning they spent journeying through the desert without saying a word.

About midday Ru'ah saw the first signs of the crop field. She was relieved that it looked just as big and beautiful as it did when they left. She could not help herself; she ran the rest of the way to it.

As she drew closer, she started to call out, "mother, mother!"

But there was no answer.

She ran throughout the field to her hut. Maybe her mother had found it and was waiting for her there.

"Mother!" she called as she approached her hut. But again, there was no answer. "Mother!" she called out a few more times. Soon Aratam joined her, but her mother was still not there. "Well, maybe she will be here tomorrow," Aratam offered. Ru'ah said nothing. She could not hide her disappointment.

The two spent the rest of the day gathering more crop and spending time together. They both knew Aratam had to leave the next day but neither of them wanted to admit it. That night they spent lying next to each other sharing stories, like they had the first night they met. Ru'ah felt so conflicted. She knew she had to stay and wait for her mother, but she could not bear the thought of not being with Aratam.

The stars shone down on them as they talked well into the night. The moon smiled down on them as they drifted off to sleep.

The next day came all too soon. Aratam had packed his bags. Ru'ah had made sure he had enough crop to last him several days.

The two walked hand and hand through the crop field and back into the desert.

"Well, my sweet Ru'ah, I suppose this is it," Aratam said.

"I suppose it is," Ru'ah sighed.

They lingered for a moment. Then Aratam wrapped Ru'ah in an embrace she would never forget. She looked up at him and pressed her lips to his. She said a silent prayer that they would find each other again soon.

As they broke apart from one another their moment was broken by an unexpected noise. They both looked to the North and saw an unexpected sight. A line of pilgrims with the insignia of Enst waving on a flag heading right towards the crop field.

Chapter Seven

Ru'ah looked up at Aratam for a clue as to what was going on, but he looked just as confused as she felt. Was this an invasion? Had they done something to anger the king? She could not fathom what that could be. As the company marched closer, Ru'ah stepped forward to meet them. Aratam followed.

"Good people on Enst, why have you come out to the desert?" Ru'ah called out.

The crowd stopped short of her and remained silent for a moment. There did not seem to be a clear leader so the atmosphere hung heavy as the members of the crowd started to shuffle and fidget. This clearly was not an insurgence after all, thought Ru'ah.

Again, she called out, "good people of Enst, why have to come out here? Is all well with the king?"

At that, a brave women stepped forward out of the crowd. "Yes, keeper of the crop, the king is well."

Ru'ah noticed the women looked as if she had seen many years. She wore a green insignia on her chest. Ru'ah remembered from her time in Enst that this was the color of the crafts people. Perhaps this woman was a fabric worker like Yri. Ru'ah was glad to hear that the king was well, but her question remained unanswered. She waited a moment to see if this woman would say anything else.

And after a moment she did, "The king has told all the kingdom of the miracle crop that healed the queen and laid the king to rest peacefully. We pilgrims were preparing to return to the temple city to pay homage to the Great Fire, but when we heard the king's tale of this great crop, we begged to see it for ourselves instead of going to the Great Fire."

Ru'ah was speechless. The king had promised to not cut off the temple city, and yet that is exactly what happened. She knew she had to tread lightly though, if she said anything disparaging about the king the pilgrims could cause a riot out here in the desert and destroy the crop. Instead, she decided to look to Aratam for help. He knew these people better than she did. Perhaps he could clarify this situation.

"Aratam, has the king gone back on his word," Ru'ah asked so that only he could hear.

"I do not think so, I think this is the people's choice," he said.

"Will you clarify, I fear I cannot bring myself to be impartial," she asked.

Aratam nodded in reply then turned to the pilgrims. "Good pilgrims it is true that the crop healed the queen and laid the king to rest in peace. Ru'ah and I were there and saw it. Yet Ru'ah is an acolyte of the Great Fire. The king had promised her to pay homage to the Great Fire, not this crop. Is it the king who has sent you here?"

The women looked reluctant to answer, but no one else stepped up. "No, keeper of the crop, we are the ones who begged to come here. The king was hesitant to allow us to come, but soon relented. We too have family members that may benefit from this crop. In all the years we have been paying homage to the Great Fire, we have never experienced a miracle like the king did. We would like that for ourselves, so we came here."

Ru'ah took in what the woman had said. Of course, the people would want to come here for their own miracle. Of course, they would want to heal their own family members. How could she deny them that? Yet, she feared what this would mean for the Great Fire, what this would mean for the people of the temple city.

She looked out at the faces of the crowd. They were all enslaved workers of the king. They all lived at the whim of someone else. They had taken a chance at begging the king for their own path and he had listened. She could not turn them away.

Ru'ah looked closer at the crowd and saw that there were indeed people in need of healing. Parents were carrying sick children; children were supporting sick parents. She saw signs of weakness and illness all around. How could she have ever mistaken this for an insurgence. Before her were people in desperate need of help. She did not want to turn them away.

She mustered up all her strength and said, “Good people, you have taken it upon yourselves to come here and you are welcome. Come, the crop is plentiful, but I ask that you only take what you need.”

With that, she stepped out of the way and let the people enter into the abundant field. She would think of a way to satisfy the Great Fire later. For now, she would give the people the same chance of survival she had been given.

Ru’ah felt Aratam grab her hand. She looked up into his eyes now filled with tears.

“Ru’ah, you went to Enst to try to save your people, and in doing so you have saved mine,” Aratam said.

She looked again at the people coming into the field through Aratam’s eyes. He had grown up with these people, probably knew most of them by name. He had been sent out on a mission from the prince that would destroy her city and possibly the known world. Instead, he found her and together they may have just saved everyone they both loved.

Ru’ah squeezed Aratam’s hand and leaned into him. She could not help but be overwhelmed at her own journey. Just a short time ago she was just an acolyte, now she was a savior. She let go of Aratam’s hand and walked around the field with the people. She watched as mothers fed the crop to their children. She joined in the amazement at the immediacy of the healings. It never ceased to amaze her how thoroughly the crop worked. She also joined in some families who held the hands of those who died after eating the crop. Death was a sting no matter what but watching a loved one die in peace was easier than watching a loved one die in pain.

The rest of the day she spent watching miracle after miracle. She cried more times than she could keep track of. All of the doubt and suffering she herself went through was worth it just to see others being healed.

As the day wore on, she noticed some families decide to leave and others setting up camp. She showed some of them how to make a hut out of the crop before herself returning to her own hut. This was by far the most emotional day she had ever experienced, and she could feel her body giving out.

Before she lay down for the night, she looked up at the stars one more time. I haven't forgotten about you mother, she thought. Perhaps tomorrow would be the day her mother would come. For now, she needed to sleep.

Ru'ah awoke to find herself laying down outside of her hut. She couldn't remember how she had gotten there. Perhaps she had sleepwalked. She had heard of that happening but had never experienced it herself. She stood up to return to her hut, but realized she was in an unfamiliar part of the field. She looked around and saw nothing but crop. There was no path, no people, no hut in sight. Where was she? She started to walk though the field but did not come across anything familiar. She was starting to become frightened when she heard a voice. It was that same sweet voice she had been waiting for.

"Ru'ah," the voice called out.

"Mother!" Ru'ah exclaimed. "Mother, you're here!"

"Ru'ah," the voice called again.

Ru'ah looked all around for a sign of where the voice was coming from. It seemed to surround her.

"Mother, where are you?" Ru'ah called out.

There was no response, so Ru'ah kept looking around. But there was nothing. No people, no path, no hut and now no voice. Once again Ru'ah became frightened. "Mother?" She called out one last time.

Defeated, she sat down in the crop field, too tired to go on. Suddenly, she heard another noise. This one was not the sweet sound of her mother's voice. It was the crackling of fire. Ru'ah looked up to see that she was completely surrounded. Her fear gave way to terror as the fire drew closer and closer, consuming the crop. She let out one scream for help and woke up safely inside her hut.

It had been another dream. She sat up to evaluate her surroundings. She was indeed inside her hut, and there did not appear to be any fire or damages. She got up to go outside. She could see hut after hut of the people who decided to stay the night.

Ru'ah looked up again at the stars. She knew in the depths of her heart that the Great Fire was coming after her. She had been sent on a mission to gather wick water to appease the Great Fire and she had failed. Instead, she had inadvertently drawn people away from the Great Fire and to this new crop. How could she?

Ru'ah thought about what the priests would do to her if they knew the truth. She was terrified. Just earlier today she had thought of herself as a savior. She was no savior; she was a traitor. She had angered the Great Fire and now it was going to seek revenge. It may even start by destroying the people she loved. She thought of Yri, Beng, Gand and the rest of the people of the city. They tried to warn her, but she hadn't listened. She was so desperate to find her mother and look what it had caused.

Why? Why hadn't she listened? Why did this crop come to her? If it was from her mother, why hadn't her mother shown up yet? Was it all a ruse? Ru'ah was questioning everything. Nothing made sense anymore. All she knew was that she had caused so much damage and she had to fix it. She looked around at all the families sleeping peacefully. Yesterday she had been thrilled to share this miracle crop, but tomorrow she would have to send everyone away. Yes, they may have been healed, but at what cost?

Tomorrow, she would set things right. Tomorrow she would turn away from the crop and go to find the wick water.

Ru'ah did not sleep the rest of the night. As much as she knew what she had to do, she dreaded having to do it. Hopefully the pilgrims who had come would be willing to go straight to Negev and stop any anger the Great Fire had until she was able to return with the wick water. She also thought about Aratam. Would he come with her? He had planned on returning to Enst, but now that there was an imminent threat maybe he would change his mind.

Ru'ah tossed and turned with all of these thoughts rushing through her mind until she saw the sun peaking up. As soon as she heard people stirring in the field, she would start sending them away.

It didn't take long. Before the sun was all the way risen the crowd from Enst was on the move. To her relief some of them looked like they were already ready to leave. So, she started making her rounds to the ones who looked content to stay.

Ru'ah came upon a family a little way down the path made up of two parents and two small children. It was unclear to her which ones had been ill since they all looked healthy now.

"I'm so sorry, but it's time for you all to go. The people of Enst must go pay homage to the Great Fire," Ru'ah said to this family. Before she could hear a response, she went to the next family to tell them they had to leave as well.

Ru'ah weaved in and out of family groups urging them to leave, not waiting for a response for the better part of the morning. She hoped that the field would be clear by midday, and she could set off herself.

As she rounded a corner to continue her mission, she felt a hand on her shoulder. Turning around she had to wait for her eyes to adjust from the shadow overcasting her. Blinking, she saw it was just Aratam. She was about to hug him but noticed the grim expression on his face.

"May I have a word," Aratam said in the same voice Ru'ah imagined he used as a palace guard.

She nodded in response and followed him as he walked out of the crop field. The further they walked the more anxious Ru'ah became. She could feel the stress coming off Aratam as well.

Once they reached the edge of the field, he turned on her.

"Why are you sending these people away?" He almost shouted at her.

She must have looked terrified because he followed up in a softer voice, "these people need the crop, why are you sending them away?"

"The Great Fire came to me in a dream last night," Ru'ah explained. "It has been angered. I must send people away and go find the wick water to appease it."

"I don't understand," Aratam said, "Why would the Great Fire be angered these people made the choice, the king did not keep them from going to the temple city."

"But they made the choice to come here. The Great Fire doesn't seem to care why people did not come to pay homage, only that people didn't come to pay homage. I'm sorry, Aratam, but I have to send people away and complete my mission, to save my people," Ru'ah said.

"But this crop has been life giving to my people," Aratam replied.

Ru'ah had never been so torn. Of course, Aratam would want his people to stay in this field. She understood where he was coming from, but she saw the bigger picture. If she did not send them away now, they could be destroyed by the Great Fire later. As difficult as it was, she had to do what she had to do.

But as she turned to go back to the crop field she was stopped in her tracks by the sounds of trumpets.

Turning back around she saw the desert start to fill with even more people holding flags with the insignia of Enst dancing in the wind.

It would seem like she would not have the crop field cleared by midday after all.

Ru'ah followed Aratam out into the desert to meet this new envoy.

"Greetings people from Enst," Aratam called out.

"Greetings Aratam, guard of the king of Enst," someone called back. Unlike yesterday's crowd this one seemed a little more organized.

"We were told you would be out here with Ru'ah, keeper of the great crop," the voice continued.

Ru'ah stepped out. "I am Ru'ah."

"Ru'ah we have orders from the king of Enst to come pay you homage," the voice called.

Had she heard right? Why would the king send people to pay her homage?

As if to answer her unasked question the voice spoke once more. "After the crowd left for the crop field yesterday from Enst, news spread of your miracle working. You came to Enst to save our King and his family. We come before you with praise and thanksgiving."

Ru'ah could not think of the words to say. Why did these people think she was the one who made the miracle?

Before she could say anything though, the new crowd rushed toward her. She could feel hands grabbing and pulling at her. This was not good, she thought to herself. She had to put an end to this quickly. She called out from Aratam to help get her out of there, but there were so many people he could not get to her. Ru'ah had not been this afraid for her life since the priests performed the coming of age ritual on her.

She continued to scramble away from the crowd but the harder she tried the closer they got to her. Soon she found she had been lifted up onto someone's shoulders.

"Praise Ru'ah, keeper of the crop!" the crowd called over and over again.

"No, this is wrong," she shouted back, but to no avail. No one could hear her over the sounds of the chants.

Ru'ah had no choice but to be carried away by the crowd. She soon found herself back in the crop field. The folks who were packing up to leave heard the commotion and decided to stay. This day was not going as planned. Ru'ah looked around desperate to get a glimpse of Aratam. Was he doing anything about the crowd, or had he joined in with them?

To her relief she was sat down by those carrying her. She watched as they turned to marvel at the crop. It was the time of day when the sun hit the stalks in just the right way that made them glisten. She could not deny that it was a sight to behold. Part of her wanted to join in with the crowd now standing in awe. Yet it was short lived. Soon the crowd dove into the crop, picking what they needed for themselves and their loved ones while they started back up the chant, "Praise Ru'ah, keeper of the crop."

In all of the chaos Ru'ah was able to sneak away to her hut. When she got inside, she had to take a deep breath to compose herself. What in the world was happening? She had never seen a crowd react like this. This would for sure anger the Great Fire more than anything else that had happened to far. She needed to think of something and quick.

She chanced a peak out of her hut to see what the crowd was up to now. To her surprise the crop had not been completely destroyed. The people were actually taking good care of it, taking only what they needed and leaving the rest for others. Some people were settling back down to eat of the crop or to just rest in its shade.

Once again Ru'ah found herself conflicted. How could she blame them to wanting to be in the presence of this crop? She had done the exact same thing. Oh, but if only they knew how much danger they were all in. Fortunately, the chanting had finally stopped. Maybe now she could think clearly.

She sat hiding in her hut watching the crowd, praying for a solution for some time when Aratam showed back up. He slipped in the hut and sat quietly beside her.

"This is quite a turn of events," he chuckled.

"I'm not sure why you find this funny," Ru'ah shot back at him. "These people are in danger, we're all in danger."

After another few moments of silence, Aratam said, "I just don't get it, why would the Great Fire be angered by people being healed, people finding peace?"

Ru'ah looked over at Aratam. She had never considered that. Why would the Great Fire be angered by this? She looked out into the crowd at the families seeing their loved ones walk for the first time in ages. She saw parents seeing their children get relief from whatever it was that had ailed them. She had to admit that she had never seen these kinds of miracles in all her time as an acolyte. This was the crop of miracles.

Yet, she was consumed with fear of the Great Fire. She had felt its power to destroy. Then, Ru'ah thought of something that truly scared her. Was the Great Fire a great, evil, fire? What kind of fire would destroy something so pure as what was happening before her? A shiver ran down her spine as she considered this new thought.

The day and come to its end and the field was still full of people. It was too late to send them away now. She would have to wait until tomorrow. For now, she needed rest. She hoped for a dreamless sleep.

Ru'ah got what she wanted. The next morning, she woke up with the sun. She felt so much better after a good night's rest, but she still had not come up with a solution to how to appease the Great Fire. After stretching she left her hut to walk around the field.

Ru'ah noticed that some people had left while others had stayed through the night. For a moment she was hopeful that by the end of the day they would have all left. As she continued walking, she was stopped occasionally by families wanting to thank her personally for the miracles they had experienced. At first, she resisted the praise. She tried to explain that she had nothing to do with any of it. But she soon realized it was easier to accept the praise graciously and then move on. No one seemed interested in her side of the story, they just needed somewhere to place their gratefulness. Maybe it was easier for them to bestow it upon her, an actual person they could talk to, instead of a plant that could not respond.

As the morning wore on, she noticed more and more people packing up to leave. This gave her a little hope, but that was soon squashed when she realized that as people were leaving, more people were coming in. It was not the same amount as the crowds from the first two days, but there was a steady trickle of new pilgrims. Would she ever be able to clear the crop field?

She found Aratam around midday eating a piece of the fruit.

"Well, I hope you're happy," Ru'ah sighed as she sat down next to him.

"I am very happy," Aratam said with all sincerity. "You should be happy too"

"How can I be happy when I know this is going to end poorly for everyone," Ru'ah exclaimed.

"You're so convinced it's going to end badly, why can't we just take a moment to enjoy the good that is happening in front of us?" Aratam responded.

Ru'ah sat with that for a moment. She really wanted to be happy, but the thought of the Great Fire's anger was holding her back.

The next few days went on much like that. Pilgrims would come to get their miracles, then they would leave, then more would come. Occasionally some of them would seek out Ru'ah to praise her. She would never get used to that, but she had come to accept it was part of her responsibility. Whether she meant to or not, she had brought these people here to the crop field. She had made its healing powers be known.

One morning, about a week after the pilgrims had first arrived Ru'ah was resting her eyes in front of her hut when a voice called out to her, "Ru'ah."

Oh that voice, the voice she had not heard in so long. She kept her eyes closed thinking it was coming from inside her head. She heard it again, 'Ru'ah."

Could it be? Ru'ah dared open her eyes and there standing before her was Yri! She looked again to see Beng and Gand with Yri as well. Was she dreaming?

"Ru'ah, it's really you!" Yri exclaimed. "I can't believe it's really you!"

"Yri, Beng, Gand," Ru'ah cried out once she was convinced that she was indeed not dreaming. "What are you doing here?"

Ru'ah was so thrilled to see her friends from the temple city that she embraced them all in the biggest hug she could muster.

She felt them embracing her back. Love pulsed through the four of them, reunited after so long. Ru'ah allowed herself to shed tears of joy.

"Oh Ru'ah we have been looking for you throughout the whole of the desert it seems," Yri continued. "It was only by luck that we found this crop field."

"If you mean by Gand's help as luck, then yes, it was by luck," Gand interrupted.

It was just like it was back in Negev. Gand hadn't changed a bit. Ru'ah looked up with loving eyes to her friend. She didn't realize how much she missed him until that moment.

"Yes, we were very lucky to have Gand leading us," Beng said as he took Ru'ah in for another hug. "And I am so glad we did."

"So, what are you doing here?" Ru'ah asked once more.

Yri's expression dropped at that question, "perhaps its best we talk in private," she said.

All at once Ru'ah feared for the worst. "Yes, we can go into my hut," she said as she led them inside.

As she did, she thought of all the times she shared with this family in their home, all the dinners and stories. She had always felt a little like an outsider, but now she was bringing them into her home, her space. They were now her guests. She sat down in her usual spot and watched as they sat down around her.

"So, can you answer my question now?" Ru'ah asked.

Yri cleared her throat but didn't speak. Ru'ah started to feel the tension growing between Yri, Beng, and Gand. It was almost as if they were daring each other to speak first.

Yri lost the dare. "We have been sent by the Chief Priests to find you and bring you back to the temple city. You have failed on your mission."

Ru'ah did not know what to say. Her greatest fears had been realized. She had chosen poorly. Now, because of her choice so many people would suffer. Because of her choice, the Great Fire would show its wrath. She put her head in her hands. But the voice, she thought, the voice assured me that no matter what choice I made it would be the right choice. Had the voice steered her wrong? Had the voice been steering her wrong this whole time. Since that night she had the first dream about her mother, she questioned whether or not it really was her mother calling her. Maybe she had been completely wrong this whole time.

Ru'ah felt a presence beside her and looked up. Yri had moved closer to her and was reaching out her arms. Ru'ah allowed herself to be held by Yri. She had missed this touch so much. She felt safe and secure for the first time in a long time.

"How long do you think I have before the city is destroyed?" Ru'ah asked.

But her question was answered only by silence.

She looked up into three confused faces.

"How long do I have?" she repeated. Maybe they hadn't heard her.

This time it was Gand who answered. "What do you mean? The city is not being destroyed."

"The Great Fire, it is angered that I have failed in my mission. That is why the priests are calling me back. Because I have failed to appease the Great Fire." Ru'ah said.

"I don't know anything about that," said Gand. "All I know is that the priests are quite angry that you have not returned. They say you have had more than enough time to complete your mission and return. They are also angry that there has been a lack of pilgrims since you left."

They didn't even know. Of course, they didn't know about the Great Fire's wrath. She had forgotten how much of a secret the Great Fire was. They didn't even know how much danger they were all in. Ru'ah started to weep once more. How could she have done this to these innocent people?

"Ru'ah," Beng said in the gently fatherly tone she loved so much. "What are all of these people doing here, in the middle of a crop field, in the middle of the desert?"

Ru'ah looked up at him. They really didn't know anything. They were simply messengers. The priests probably sent them because they knew she would return with them. Ru'ah decided they had a right to know the whole truth. These people had practically raised her, they had welcomed her into their home and loved her. They had been sent on this mission because of their love for her. So, she wiped away her eyes and told them everything.

Ru'ah told them of her journey in the desert, and how she had given up hope. She told them about the crop field, how it was the same one from her dreams. She told them about her mother and Aratam. She told them all about the prince and how these pilgrims where here to pay homage to the crop and gather their own miracles. When she had finished her tale, she was exhausted by all that has happened. She could tell by their expressions they were a little exhausted as well.

“All of that happened in three months?” Yri said.

“Has it really only been three months? Honestly, I’ve lost track of time out here,” Ru’ah said.

“Three short months,” said Yri, “and now it is time for you to return.”

“Yes, I suppose you are right. I have not found what I was looking for, but I cannot hide away forever,” Ru’ah said. Perhaps Aratam was right, perhaps freedom is too difficult. She had thought she had found her own, but she saw now that freedom came with too much of a cost. If she stayed here in the crop field so many others would suffer. She had to return.

“Before we leave, I would like to show you my crop, show you its power,” Ru’ah said.

Yri, Beng, and Gand agreed to look around. “But we must leave as soon as we can, the desert is not a safe place,” said Gand.

Once they saw the crop, they would understand that they were in a safe place, thought Ru’ah. She brought them out of the hut and into the field. “It is a crop of miracles. It can heal, but we have learned that healing means different things for different people. Sometimes it can mean curing the sick, sometimes it can mean feeding the hungry, and sometimes it can mean a peaceful death.”

Ru’ah handed pieces of fruit to her friends and waited to see what would happen. At first, they were hesitant, not quite trusting what was before them. They once again looked at each other to see who would go first.

Beng was the first to go. He took a small bite, but Ru’ah could see the affects taking hold. His eyes lit up and soon finished his whole piece. “This is unlike anything I have ever had before. All the pain in my back and legs are gone, but more than that I feel … at peace,” he said.

With that reassurance both Yri and Gand ate of their fruits. They too had similar experiences. “This is unbelievable, it is the most delicious thing I have ever eaten," said Yri. "Yes, and I do feel healed and at peace," said Gand. "It's like a load I've been carrying has been lifted. It's like I now have the courage to do things I couldn't before."

"Do you see now why I have been here?" Ru'ah asked. "This crop is my crop. It is my mother's crop, whenever she shows up. I will return with you, but I needed you to know why I stayed."

Ru'ah was about to return to her hut to gather her few belongings when Aratam run up to her. "Ru'ah new pilgrims have arrived and wish to speak with you."

Ru'ah was torn. She longed to greet these new pilgrims but knew Yri, Beng, and Gand were waiting for her.

"It is alright, Ru'ah. We can wait," Yri said.

This was certainly a change from the tension she felt in the hut. Perhaps the crop had calmed all of their nerves. Ru'ah followed Aratam to these new pilgrims and soon found herself distracted with more and more pilgrims wanting to speak with her, pay her homage, or just ask her questions about the crop. She could not turn away from them. She knew how incredible the crop was, especially to people who were experiencing it for the first time.

By the time she returned to the family from the temple city the sun was well into setting. It was too late to leave for the day. They would have to wait until morning.

"I am sorry, it is so hard to turn away these pilgrims. I have tried." Ru'ah said.

"Believe it or not, after tasting this crop, we understand. It is hard for us to leave now," said Gand.

Ru'ah was so glad to hear that they felt the same way. She was grateful for Gand's honesty. She could always count on him to speak truth, even if it was a difficult truth. Ru'ah realized just how much she missed this family. In the back of her mind, she hoped they could all stay in the crop field forever.

Ru'ah awoke the next day to find the sun well into rising, but Yri, Beng, and Gand were nowhere to be found. Had they left without her?

Ru'ah rushed out of her hut but didn't have to go far to find the three family members sitting with Aratam chatting away like old friends.

"Hello," Ru'ah said as she approached the group.

"She rises!" said Gand. "We thought we'd let you sleep a little after all this hard work you've been doing.

"Oh, thank you," Ru'ah said. "I will eat some fruit and then I will be ready to leave with you all."

"There's no rush, we are in the middle of sharing stories," Aratam said.

This was a surprise. She knew they all loved stories, so she was pleased to join them. All morning they went around sharing stories of their lives, and stories of old. Occasionally they would be interrupted by pilgrims wishing to speak with Ru'ah, but then they would go right back into their tales. Ru'ah was pleased to see Aratam and Gand getting along so well. These two were her closest friends. The only thing that would make this moment better was if her mother would show up. But that still did not happen.

Before long, Ru'ah realized it would once again be too late to leave that day, and once again, they would have to wait until morning. She did not say anything, but she was pleased by this as well.

The next several days went like this. Yri, Beng, and Gand would find some excuse not to leave, and Ru'ah would go along with it. She had a feeling they wanted to stay just as much as she did. Soon they all lost track of how long they had been there.

One morning as Ru'ah, Yri, Beng, Gand, and Aratam were sitting down for their morning meal, as had become their custom, Yri pulled Ru'ah aside.

"Ru'ah, this is a miracle crop," Yri said.

"Yes, I know," Ru'ah replied.

"This is the miracle crop. Beng, Gand and I were speaking about it last night and agree – this is the true miracle. The Great Fire has never done anything like this before. We will not make you return to the priests. We wish to not return to the priests as well," Yri said.

Ru'ah was stunned. She had thought that herself for some time but never would have said it out loud. But, hearing Yri say it filled her with assurance that they should indeed stay in this crop field, where they belonged.

Ru'ah pulled Yri into a hug. "I am so happy to hear that. Yes, we will all stay here with the crop. We will find a way to spread the news of this crop far and wide!"

The two women joined in with the new family to eat of this most wonderful meal.

As they finished up and were preparing for the rest of the day, they heard quite the commotion coming from the outskirts of the field. Ru'ah feared what she would find as she rushed over to the noise. What she found filled her with dread.

There, right outside her crop field, were the Chief Priests Iddo and Yawen demanding for Ru'ah's to show herself.

Chapter Eight

"Ah, there you are," Iddo said when she spotted Ru'ah coming out of the crop field.

Ru'ah felt the air fly out of her lungs. Seeing her former masters in her crop field was the last thing she expected. Not only was Ru'ah worried what their presence here meant for her, she also knew that since they were so attached to the temple and the city, leaving it must mean danger had come. Had the Great Fire started its destruction already?

Before she could stop herself, Ru'ah started to kneel before the Chief Priests. "Chief priests Iddo and Yawen, how can I serve you," Ru'ah said. But before they could answer she stood back up. She did not have to bow to them, they were in her field now. She was no longer under their control. She was free. Free from them, free from their expectations of her, free to herself. She saw the stunned expressions on their faces when she rose to her full height. They clearly were not expecting such a response from her. Instead of being intimidated by this, though, Ru'ah found her courage rising.

"Iddo and Yawen, Chief Priests of the Great Fire, welcome to the crop of miracles," Ru'ah said.

Yawen's eyes bore into her. "This is no crop of miracles, this is nonsense," he said.

"Ru'ah acolyte of the Chief Priests, you have failed in your mission to retrieve the wick water as was requested. You must return with us now and face the consequences," Iddo said.

"Chief Priests, I have indeed failed in my mission to retrieve the wick water, but in my failure, I have found something even more powerful. I have found this crop of miracles and have shared it with all these people. This crop is one of healing. I ask, before you leave to taste of it and see for yourself," said Ru'ah.

She had never seen the priests look so indignant, as if the very sight of this crop offended them to their core. Yet she stood firm. There was not an ounce of herself left that was afraid of them. She was free now and would never blindly obey them again.

"You would do well to stop this pretense," said Yawen. "You are causing more harm that you could ever imagine."

"You fear the Great Fire will be offended by this crop, but I know this crop's true powers. Nothing good would be offended by it," said Ru'ah.

"You do not know what you say," said Yawen, his eyes blazing with wrath.

Ru'ah did not stand down even then. She thought back to the many times this look from Yawen would have sent her into a death spiral. He used to have so much power over her. She was once again amazed at how much had changed.

It was then that Ru'ah noticed Iddo and Yawen were not alone. They had brought with them several scouts. Along with them was Tell, the Wise Scout. Ru'ah had to admit that Tell looked more intimidating than the Chief Priests. Although she was a scout, she looked like a warrior, come here to protect her masters.

Ru'ah wasn't sure what her next steps should be. She did not want to cause any reason for Tell and the rest of the scouts to act, but she knew she could not budge in her position either.

She watched as Yawen turned from her to the scouts. If he was going to give them orders to capture her, she had to act fast. She needed to get the upper hand. She thought about Yri, Beng, and Gand. She would need to protect them from the priests' wrath as well. They had defied orders too after all. Where was Aratam? Perhaps he could get them to safety. She would need to get the pilgrims to safety as well. Would the crop field come to their aid? It had provided for them so far. Yawen was just about to open his mouth to give an order, Ru'ah was just about to make her move to find her friends. It all came down to this split second for her. She knew how powerful the priests could be. She knew the scouts would not hesitate to follow orders.

"Wait," Iddo said just loud enough to get everyone's attention. Yawen turned to her with fire in his eyes. Ru'ah knew he was not used to being stopped, not even from his partner.

"Wait for what?" he said.

"It is time she knew," Iddo interrupted. Yawen turned to Iddo and considered her words. Ru'ah watched Iddo and Yawen have a silent conversation, the way only two people who knew each other deeply could do. Yawen clearly did not want to turn away from him plan, but Iddo had something else in mind. What that something else was, Ru'ah had no idea.

Slowly, Yawen gave in to Iddo's will. He nodded his agreement and stood down.

Iddo approached Ru'ah. "It is time you knew the truth. Yet, it cannot be revealed here, there are too many others listening. We must go somewhere private."

Against her better judgment Ru'ah started to lead Iddo towards the field and to her hut. She noticed that Yri, Beng, Gand, and Aratam had been standing behind her the whole time. Even though she feared for their safety, she felt safer knowing her friends were so close by.

Ru'ah was even more comforted when Yri started walking right beside them. Yri would have known the punishment for being insubordinate to the Chief Priests could be cruel, yet she still stood by Ru'ah side against the power of Iddo. Ru'ah thought how wonderful it was to have such a friend.

As they walked through the field Ru'ah stopped once in a while to greet the pilgrims and answer some of their questions.

"Ru'ah, keeper of the crop, we thank you with all that we have for this miracle. Our daughter is able to speak with us as she has never done before," a man said as Ru'ah walked by. She reached out a hand to him, but did not say anything. She was still not sure how to respond to people who wished to put the praise on her, but she felt it was crucial for Iddo to see how important this crop was to all these people.

She could feel Iddo's glare each time she stopped, but that did not discourage her. Her friends also remained close by, never straying far from her. Yet, Yawen did not follow. As far as Ru'ah knew, he was still standing just outside of the crop field with the scouts. She wandered what the scouts would do with all the pilgrims. Surely they would not try to clear the whole field while she was with Iddo.

Once the group reached her hut, she invited Iddo in. But one look from the Chief Priests told the rest of the group to remain outside. The two women sat down across from each other. Ru'ah offered Iddo a piece of fruit, but she refused. Ru'ah took a generous bite and waited to hear what Iddo had to say. "You know about the Great Fire, you know that long ago the fire consumed the earth, yet in its benevolence it made the desert. Through the desert came humanity, and soon humanity learned how to appease the Great Fire. The first Chief Priests brought the Great Fire into the temple and since then, Chief Priests have tended to it, offering sacrifice and paying homage on behalf of all the people. For generations now this is what has kept the Great Fire satisfied. Do you understand the importance of what I am saying?" Iddo said.

Ru'ah stared blankly. She had heard most of this already, but wasn't sure where Iddo was going with it.

"The importance is tradition. Doing the same rituals, passing down the same ways of doing things from generation to generation. It is the only way we can be sure the Great Fire will remain benevolent. If things change, if tradition is broken, we cannot guarantee anyone is safe. We must keep up tradition. Since you have failed to retrieve the wick water, you have failed tradition."

Ru'ah was now completely lost. Hadn't she been sent the wick water to appease the Fire from the prince's treats? How was that breaking tradition? Her face must have given her thoughts away. Iddo continued: "When the acolyte comes of age they are put through the traditional ritual of the Great Fire. They are told the story, shown the Great Fire, and given as a sacrifice. All that you did. Yet, what was unexpected was how much emotion you showed when presented with the Great Fire. Do you remember that?"

Ru'ah thought back. That's what she had done that was so unexpected? She had cried in front of the Great Fire. But how could she not have, she was so moved by it. She thought back to how Yawen had reacted, he was stoic. "I was supposed to be unmoved by it," Ru'ah said.

"Yes, the new priest is supposed to be in control of their feelings around the Great Fire. If you are not, it can easily overpower you. Yawen and I knew we needed to drain you of your emotion. And so, we sent you on this mission of find wick water."

Ru'ah felt her legs going numb, she needed to shift her position. She also needed a moment to process what Iddo had just said. She stood up to walk around the hut. She wanted to get as far away from Iddo as possible, far away from what she was saying. Ru'ah tugged at her clothes, grateful she was not any more constrained in her traveling clothes. She wondered what the priests thought of her hand made clothes. They must have been shocked by them, but maybe not anymore shocked than finding her in this field. After walking around the hut a few times, she realized she couldn't avoid this conversation with Iddo any longer. Sitting back down and taking a breath she asked, "I thought the mission for wick water was to appease the Great Fire from the prince's threats?"

"Ah, no that was only good timing. The prince posed a challenge to be sure, but we have other ways of dealing with wayward princes. Your mission was meant to strip you of emotion," said Iddo.

"How? How would wick water strip me of emotion?"

"There is no wick water. The meaning of the mission if for you to be broken down so you return to the temple fully prepared to serve the Great Fire alone, instead of being swayed by emotions," said Iddo.

Ru'ah felt the truth of this revelation wash over her, her worst fears realized. She had been sent on a fool's errand. The priests had kept her naive, how much else had they lied about? Ru'ah had to stand back up. She had to get out of this hut, it was too small for both of them. The longer Iddo stayed in it, the less it felt like her home. She needed her freedom back. Walking around didn't help as much as she had hoped. She sat back down but couldn't look at Iddo. She felt tears start to form but fought them back. She would not let the priests see her cry, she would not let them think they were breaking her, like they intended. She could never be stoic like they wanted her to be, but she refused to satisfy them with her emotions, those were for her and her alone.

Iddo must have become impatient with Ru'ah because she continued speaking, "The journey out in the desert was meant to strip you bare. Make you rid yourself of all emotions, so that you can come back stronger. The desert was meant to make you a better priest to the Great Fire. Instead, it has caused all kinds of havoc."

Ru'ah looked around her hut. Her hut that was made out of this miracle crop. She was sent out into the desert to fail for the Great Fire, instead this crop field saved her life.

"I don't understand, my mother sent me this crop field. How could this be havoc? How can any of this be true?"

"Your mother?" Iddo asked.

"My mother sent me a message in a dream that she was waiting for me in this field. When I was at the brink of death out in this desert she brought this crop to me to save me," Ru'ah said.

"Ru'ah, don't you get it. The priesthood has been passed down from generation to generation all the way from the first Chief Priests. Each generation has one child who is made acolyte. When that child comes of age they are put through the ritual sacrifice to become the new Chief Priest. Once they are fully prepared the old Chief Priests remove themselves. The new Chief Priest chooses a united partner to produce the next acolyte who will continue the tradition. Ru'ah you are the acolyte. Yawen was the former acolyte and chose me to be his untied partner. Yawen is your father, and I am your mother."

Time stood still. Ru'ah felt her heartbeat stop, her blood freeze, her senses shut off. Everything around her became a blur. She couldn't tell if she was sitting up or laying down. She couldn't tell if she was awake or dreaming. Everything she had ever known had been changed forever. After the initial shock wore off, she took a deep breath. She had to fight hard to keep the tears from falling. How could this be? She was so unlike the priests; she had never felt anything other than obligation to them. They had never shown her anything other than necessity. Yet she was supposed to believe they were her parents? It was true they were the ones who fed her, gave her a place to stay, took care of her basic needs, but parents were supposed to be more than that. She looked outside of her hut for a moment. She needed something to grasp, something to make it all make sense. She saw Yri and Beng out in the distance. Her friends, the family that had claimed her. They were the ones who cared for her. They were the ones she turned to when she needed love. Not the priests. No, it couldn't be the priests. But, the more Ru'ah thought, the more she knew Iddo was telling the truth. The way the people of the city reacted to her, always giving her exactly what she asked for, always saving the best products for her. She thought about her coming of age celebration and how afterwards people looked at her with reverence. She knew she was the daughter of Iddo and Yawen, Chief Priests of the Great Fire.

But what could she say? What else could be said. She looked again out at Yri and Beng.

"Do they know who I am?" Ru'ah asked. It was the only thing she could think of to say.

"Yes, everyone in the temple city knows who you are," said Iddo.

"Is that why they took me in, because they knew I wouldn't have a real family?"

"No, not exactly," said Iddo. "The new Chief Priest chooses their united partner. But that chosen partner gets honor and privilege themselves. Yri and Beng took you in so that you would choose their son, Gand as your united partner."

This was more than Ru'ah could bear. Her whole life had really been a lie. The people she thought truly loved her really only cared about their own position. No wonder they tried so hard to keep her within their family. They made sure she was happy with them, not because they cared about her but so that she would care about them. What did that mean about Aratam? She always saw Gand as a brother, but she felt so strongly for Aratam. Did he only see her for her position as well? Nothing made sense, nothing was right. Ru'ah felt herself stand up. She couldn't see or think straight. All she knew was that she had to get out of that hut, she had to get away from Iddo, from the false life she had. She ran. She ran past the pilgrims eating the crop. She ran past Yri, Beng, Gand and even Aratam. She ran though the field, the field she once thought was a miracle. She ran and ran until she could not run anymore.

She no longer knew anything. Was this field a crop of miracles, or was it just more lies? Who was it that had visited her in a dream? It was not her mother after all. Her mother was the Chief Priest. She was the daughter of the Chief Priest. She was not another enslaved worker. She was the next Chief Priest of the Great Fire.

The Great Fire – that day she had admitted she no longer believed in the it. She had claimed the crop as the real worker of miracles. She had been wrong, wrong about everything. She really had cursed all of humanity to suffer. Maybe this crop was nothing but poison after all. Maybe the Great Fire was poison as well and there was nothing good in the world. That would make as much sense as anything else. The Great Fire and this crop field had caused her so much pain, so much suffering in this short amount of time, of course it could be poison. It was her poison at least.

Ru'ah felt her body tingling. She needed to do something, anything to rid her body of this deep hurt. She needed to hurt something. She grabbed a stalk. She had been so hesitant to pull them out just a little while ago. She had wanted to preserve them so that all could enjoy their healing power. But now, she wanted them gone forever. She pulled with all her might. She could defeat this crop. She would not let it poison anyone else. She pulled and pulled, but it would not come out of the ground. Ru'ah went to another stalk, but it too would not pull up. She tried over and over again to destroy the crop, but nothing she did worked.

Finally too exhausted to go on, Ru'ah fell onto the ground. She had not been so spent since the crop field appeared to her. How was she to go on now? She wanted so badly to curse the crop field, curse Iddo and Yawen, even curse Yri, Bend, and Gand. But she couldn't. All she could do was cry.

And just like the moment before the crop field surrounded her all that time ago, she did cry, she cried and cried until she could cry no more. She let emotions take control and she was stripped bare. Ru'ah, acolyte of the Great Fire, keeper of the crop field, was defeated.

When the last tear shed, she looked up into the sky. The sun was still shining so there were no stars, but she couldn't help but think of them. Her mother, or the one she thought had been her mother, told her she knew how many stars were in the sky. Was that a lie as well? Was it really just a dream after all? But the crop field had turned out to be real. Nothing made sense. Nothing would make sense every again, Ru'ah thought.

The longer she stared up into the sky the more she thought she could see stars. They were very faint at first, but the more she looked, the clearer they became. Soon the sky was completely dark, and the stars shone bright. Has she been sitting there for that long? Had no one come to look for her? Did no one care that she had been gone, not even Aratam?

Just as she had thought that, she felt someone sit down beside her. Perhaps Aratam had shown up after all. Ru'ah looked over to her friend only to see it was not her friend there at all.

"Ru'ah, why are you crying?"

It was the voice, that beautiful voice she had been looking for this whole time. The voice, the being with the voice had come to her.

"You're here, finally!" Ru'ah said.

"No, you are here, finally," said the voice.

"What?" said Ru'ah.

"You are here. I have been here the whole time, waiting for you," said the voice.

Ru'ah looked around to see if she was still in the crop field. As far as she could tell, she was.

"I don't understand," she said.

"Ru'ah, I have been here since before the beginning of time. It is you I have been waiting for," said the voice.

"So, this is your crop field after all?"

"This is my crop field; this is my world."

"I really don't understand," said Ru'ah.

The voice took a deep breath, as if she was about to explain something she had explained many times before.

"Ru'ah I am the one that made the crop field, I am the one that made the Great Fire, I am the one that made you, I am the one that made this whole earth. I have been here the whole time, I will be here the whole time. I have been waiting for you, and now you are here."

"Why have you been waiting for me?" asked Ru'ah.

"I wait for all my children," said the voice.

"So, you are my mother? Iddo was lying?"

"You are my child, and Iddo is my child. And Yawen and Yri and Beng and Gand and Aratam and every person in this world is my child. The stars are my children. That is how I know how many there are, just like how I know how many you are."

"So Iddo and Yawen really are my parents. I really am meant to be the next Chief Priest of the Great Fire," said Ru'ah.

"What you are meant to do is up to you. But the intention of your parents is that you will become the next Chief Priest of the fire."

"Is that why you came to me, to prepare me for this role?" asked Ru'ah.

"No, I came to you because you needed me. I come to all my children who need me in one way or another."

"How did you know I needed you. I didn't even know I needed you."

"I know more about you than you even know about yourself. You must trust me on that one."

Ru'ah tried to resist, but she had to admit that she trusted the voice implicitly.

"Then why did I need you?"

"You were lost, you were doubting, and so I came to you, to reassure you," said the voice.

"To reassure me of the power of the Great Fire?" asked Ru'ah.

"No, to reassure you of me."

For a moment Ru'ah looked at the being the voice was coming from, but soon had to look away, she was so beautiful.

"Long ago the people of this world needed fire, and so I gave them fire. But I try not to interfere too much in their affairs. I find that people accept my gifts better when they don't realize it is me giving it to them. This fire gave them warmth, and good food to eat. But, the humans misunderstood the gift. They soon saw the fire not as a tool but as a being worthy of worship. For years now they have been giving sacrifices and paying homage to something that was only meant to serve them. There have been those who show doubt in the great fire, yet the tradition is so strong, their doubt is met with threats. Whole societies have been constructed around this great fire.

Those with power oppress others in the name of the great fire. Is any of this sounding familiar?"

Stunned at the accuracy of what the voice was saying, Ru'ah could only nod her head in agreement.

"My heart would break any time one of my children suffered at the hand of another one of my children in the name of this gift freely given. But I love my children, all of my children, and so I have decided to give them another gift." The voice gestured at the crop.

"So the crop is good?" asked Ru'ah.

"Yes, the crop is good. As you have discovered it is for the healing of all people. And as you have discovered, healing means different things to different people. My desire is that all people are able to come and taste the sweetness of this crop."

"Is that why you chose me?"

"Ru'ah I did not choose you. You were in need and so I provided for you. But, now that you know the trust of this crop my hope is that you will spread this truth. I hope you will continue to welcome all people to this field to come and be healed. My hope is that you will use this truth to turn society away from oppression where some rule over others. This is a job not easily done, and you will need help. But my hope is that you will trust me when I say you can do this."

Ru'ah thought for a moment. It was true that she had the desire to spread this news. And she knew it was true she would need help. But who could she trust, she just found out that everyone she thought she could trust had lied to her.

The voice must have been able to read her mind because it said, "Iddo has lived in this tradition her whole life. When she was a child, she was raised to be the partner of the Chief Priest. Her parents made that choice for her. She cannot understand that some parents allow their children to make their own choices. She cannot understand that some parents want what's best for their children, even if their children are not born to them."

Ru'ah considered these words. She considered the memory of when Yri founded her in the market for the first time. Although she had been just a small child, she felt no ulterior motives. All she remembered feeling from Yri was love. That is all she ever felt from Yri and Beng. They had invited her to their home, fed her from their table. She had grown up playing with Gand as a brother. Never once had she felt pressure to be more than that.

She considered how Gand looked at her on the night of her coming of age. Perhaps he really had been taken by her, but it was not the same way Aratam looked at her. She did not look at Gand the same way she looked at Aratam. Gand was not for her, and she was not for Gand. She truly believed Yri and Beng knew that, but she asked anyway, "are you saying Yri and Beng were not trying to lead Gand and me to each other? They really did care about me?"

"I will not reveal the hearts of others, but I can tell you that you can trust the love you already share with your family," said the voice.

"I don't have a family. Unless you count the priests as my parents."

"Ru'ah family does not always mean the people you were born to. Family is the people you love and who love you."

"So what do I do now?" Ru'ah asked. She was afraid she had asked too many questions but the voice never wavered in its sweet, patient tone. It still spoke as if Ru'ah was the most important person in the world. That made Ru'ah feel more loved than she had ever felt before.

"Let us just sit her for a while with one another," the voice said.

Ru'ah liked the sound of that. And that is what they did. For minutes, or a lifetime Ru'ah sat next to this being. She was not her mother; she was so much more.

After however long, Ru'ah felt it was time to depart form this place, wherever this place was. She turned to the voice.

"I'm ready."

"I know you are."

"But one more thing before I go," asked Ru'ah.

The voice nodded, still so patient.

"What is your name?"

The voice looked like she had never considered this question before.

"I have had many names throughout the history of the world. Some of them I like better than others. I have never given myself a name since I have never felt the need for one, I just am who I am. What would you like to call me?"

Ru'ah knew exactly how to answer that question, "I would like to call you Miracle."

The voice smiled, "Yes, I like that."

Ru'ah stood up to walk back to her hut. "I am ready," she said.

"I know you are," said Miracle.

The stars were no longer shining, rather the sun was high in the sky. Ru'ah made her way back to find her family. Together they would share the truth of this Miracle.

Yri, Beng, Gand, and Aratam were still outside of the hut when Ru'ah came back. Yri ran up to her and pulled her into a tight hug. Ru'ah felt love surging between them and she wrapped her arms around her surrogate mother. Before long, the rest of the group joined in the hug.

"I know everything know. I know I am the daughter of the Chief Priests. I know what my life was going to be," Ru'ah said.

"We wanted to tell you so many times," said Yri. "But we were sworn to secrecy. The whole city was."

"I know that now. And I know that you loved me and did your best to take care of me," said Ru'ah.

She let go of the group hug and turned to Gand. "Gand, I have loved you as a brother, and know you have loved and protected me as your sister."

Gand's smile outshone the sun. "It is true. I have been so proud to walk with you throughout this life. I have never wanted anything but the best for you. I saw how beautiful you were at your coming of age party, and I see how beautiful and strong you are now. I will forever be at your service."

Ru'ah pulled Gand into another hug. She was so proud to call him her brother.

"You are my family, all of you," Ru'ah said, turning to Aratam. "You have only recently come into my life, but I feel like I have known you forever. You are my kindred spirit. I hope you will consider staying with us."

Aratam blinked back tears, "Nothing would make me happier," he said.

Ru'ah pulled them all back into a hug. She had waited so long on a mother who would never come, but she had found something so much more. She was finally with the family who would love her no matter what.

"Now, I am ready to face Iddo again. Will you all come with me into the hut?"

"We will go with you wherever you ask us to go," said Beng. "But, Iddo is no longer in the hut. After you ran out, she return to Yawen without a word."

"Does that mean they left?" asked Aratam.

"Not likely," said Beng. "I think it means they are planning something."

"Yes, before Iddo stopped him, Yawen was going to ask the scouts to do something. I fear we may all be in danger," said Ru'ah.

"Well, let us go face this danger together," said Gand.

Ru'ah grabbed Gand and Aratam's hands. Yri and Beng joined in. Together they walked through the crop field to face whatever the priests had in store.

Chapter Nine

As Ru'ah and her chosen family walked through the field, they could see the pilgrims' worried expressions. Ru'ah wanted to run, but she stopped occasionally to comfort these frightened faces. They had come all this way for the healing crop; she would not let them leave worse off.

"We need to get the pilgrims to safety," she said to the group. "Tell everyone to get as far back in the field as they can."

Without hesitation, they all did as she said. Yri and Beng went to the families with small children to help them get up and moving. Gand and Aratam helped those with older family members who could not move quickly. Soon the pilgrims were helping each other as well. Before long Ru'ah did not see anyone else between her and the path to the priests. She hoped the way would remain clear.

Yri, Beng, Gand, and Aratam rejoined her. As they continued to march to the priests Ru'ah smelled something in the air that filled her with dread. It was smoke. But not any smoke. This was the smoke that had once filled the temple where she served. The priests had brought the Great Fire with them.

As one, the group sped up to reach the edge of the crop field. They took their last step out into the open. Ru'ah sent a silent prayer to Miracle for protection and strength.

"I'm ready," Ru'ah said as she came face to face once again with the priests.

"Iddo and Yawen, Chief Priests of the Great Fire, you have come to my crop field to bring me back to the temple city. I refuse to go. I welcome you to stay, but if you do, you will pay respect to this crop, and listen to what I have to say."

Yawen had been crouched down by the edge of the field. As Ru'ah spoke he stood up, revealing what he had planned. The scouts had brought with them kindling. Yawen had in his hands the flame of the Great Fire. He was going to burn the crop field down.

"I will not listen to anything you have to say. You have chosen to betray tradition, and for that you must pay," Yawen said.

He then gave a signal to the scouts, who were now in full warrior mode. Tell, along with three other scouts rushed at Ru'ah. Gand and Aratam jumped in front of her in order to stop them, but they were no match. The warriors overtook them. Tell herself grabbed Ru'ah. She resisted with all her might but Tell had trained for this. Tell would not disappoint her master.

Ru'ah called out to Yri and Beng to run, but they stood steadfast. Aratam and Gand had been knocked out. She saw the warriors getting rope to tie them up. Yri and Beng ran to their son's defense, but they too were defeated. Ru'ah and just found this family, she could not lose them.

"Tell, please I ask you to listen to what I have to say. I know the truth and I want to share it with you. We don't have to do this; we don't have to be anyone's slave. I know the truth of freedom" Ru'ah said.

She saw a flash in Tell's eyes. Had she convinced her? No, it wouldn't be that easy. Tell tied Ru'ah up as had been her command. The other warriors came over to help carry Ru'ah to the pile of kindling. The priests were going to burn her along with this crop.

Ru'ah thought of all the pilgrims hiding out. She looked at her friends, her family, tied up and gaged. This was not what she had wanted at all. She could not fail all of these people.

Yawen raised the flame of the Great Fire up for all to see.

"Ru'ah acolyte of the Chief Priests of the Great Fire, you have failed," he shouted. "You were raised to be the next Chief Priest, but you abandoned that call. You abandoned your family; you abandoned the Great Fire itself. You have brought shame to this world by the worship of this false idol. You have angered the Great Fire, and now you must perish."

Yawen chanted a prayer of sacrifice Ru'ah had heard many times before. She could chant along with him, but instead she looked up. The stars were just now coming out in the night sky. She started to count them. And then she smiled.

Ru'ah took a deep breath, then called at the top of her lungs, "Miracle. Miracle."

Yawen stopped only for a moment to consider her last words. Iddo had joined him but refused to look up at Ru'ah.

As Yawen and Iddo together lowered the flame to the kindling, the night sky went dark. The stars were no more. Heavy clouds had filled the sky and rain began pouring down.

Ru'ah smiled as she watched this eternal flame of the Great Fire that had been preserved throughout the generations go out with a single drop of water.

For a moment all was silent. No one dare move a muscle. Ru'ah watched as Iddo and Yawen looked at one another as if to see what the other would do. Ru'ah knew how earth shattering this would be for the priests. She dared not say anything yet, so as to avoid further wrath. They, of course, would blame this on her. She looked over at the warriors and her friends. They all had the same dumbfounded expressions of their faces. While Yri, Beng, Gand, and Aratam where on her side, they would still be shocked to see the Great Fire defeated so easily. They too would be anxious to see how the priests reacted.

Tell was not too far away. She would have had a direct view. She was now standing at the ready for her next orders, but Ru'ah could see Tell was just as shaken.

As Ru'ah suspected, Yawen turned to the crowd and immediately blamed her. "This temptress has made it so that it seems the Great Fire has been put out, but I assure you it is only a mirage. The Great Fire is in control and revenge will be swift."

His words did not do much to persuade the audience. But the warriors shook off their dismay to be at the ready.

"Tell, have your troops pluck this crop right out of the ground!" Yawen commanded.

Tell hesitated, but then gave the nod to the rest of the warriors. They moved as one to the crop field. Ru'ah was interested to see if they would fare any better than she had when she tried to pull the crop up.

She bit back a laugh as she watched the warriors struggle. Despite all their effort and training, the crop would not even budge. Ru'ah felt an unfamiliar sensation welling up inside her. Miracle was nearby. She looked around but could not see her anywhere. Then it occurred to her. Miracle was here, and always would be. Miracle was within Ru'ah and within the crop field. Miracle was giving Ru'ah the courage she needed to share what she knew.

"Chief Priests of the Great Fire; Warriors of the Chief Priests, I ask you once again to listen to what I have to say," Ru'ah said.

The warriors continued their mission. They would not stop until their masters gave them the command. Ru'ah was about to repeat herself when she made eye contact with Tell. Ru'ah could sense that Tell wanted to listen to her, so she made her move. "Tell, you have served the Chief Priests your whole life as a desert scout. You know better than anyone that this crop should not be here. The desert is not suitable for this kind of growth. You have known me my whole life, you know how dedicated I was to the service of the Great Fire. You must believe that if I say this crop is good, it is good."

Tell looked at Ru'ah for a little while longer.

"If you won't trust her, you should at least trust me," Gand called out. "I have tasted the crop and I can say that it is good."

This pushed Tell over the edge. "Scouts, warriors, let us listen," she called out.

The scouts were well trained. Once again, they moved as one to stand back behind Tell.

Yawen tried to give them orders, but his commands were no good. The rain continued to pour on the company as they prepared to listen to what Ru'ah had to say.

"Long ago, before time began there was nothing except the creator. In time, the creator started to do what she does best – she created. She created the desert and all that is in it. The creator created us human. She even created the Great Fire itself," Ru'ah started.

"These are lies, she is telling you all lies," Yawen shouted.

Gand and Aratam, who had managed to escape from their bondage surrounded Yawen. Their presence was enough to make him lower his voice, especially since the warrior scouts made no attempt to protect him.

When Yawen had settled down, Ru'ah continued. "The creator made the great fire so that humans would have warmth. They could use the great fire to prepare food and be clean. The great fire was a gift to us humans. But, we misunderstood. We thought it was the great fire that gave us these things. We thought we were made for the great fire. And so, long ago two people became the Chief Priests of the fire, convincing others that if they paid homage and sacrificed to the great fire, it would protect them. They did not understand it was them who could decide the fate of the great fire.

They made a temple for the great fire. They made societies based on the great fire. These societies had an order, with the Chief Priests at the top, the kings and queens next, and the rest of us humans enslaved at the bottom. This was not what the creator intended. We humans did this to one another in the name of the great fire, the gift given to us.

For years now, generations have passed down this type of society. For generations we have paid homage and sacrifice to this great fire. For generations we have lived as enslaved workers to the priests and kings simply because that it what we have always known. But I say to you now, it does not have to be this way. We have each been made as children of the creator. Not one of us is made to be the slave of the other. We can change the way we live. And I know that the creator wants that."

Ru'ah paused to see if anyone was still following her.

Tell called out, "how do you know all of this?"

This was the part Ru'ah had been worried about. How was she going to convince this crowd that the creator herself had spoken to her? Why would they believe that?

Ru'ah took a deep breath and felt Miracle's encouraging presence. She would have to trust that they would.

"When I came of age, not that long ago, I had a dream. In this dream I was transported to a crop field and met the most amazing being I have ever seen. Her voice alone made me want to weep with joy. She spoke to me of the stars, telling me she knew how many there were in the sky. She told me she was the one I wanted her most to be. At the time I thought she was my mother, but it turns out she was so much more."

"She was the creator," Yri said. "I have had dreams where I have heard that same voice calling my name."

Ru'ah saw many in the crowd nodding in agreement. It was as if they all knew exactly what she was talking about. Emboldened, she continued.

"When the Chief Priests sent me out into the desert to find wick water for the Great Fire, I came to a point that I was so exhausted I could not go on. That was when the crop appeared around me. I ate of its yield and my life was spared. So many of us have tasted the fruit and have had the same experience. Even the King of Enst has had that experience. That is why all these pilgrims are here, to experience their own miracles.

This is what the creator wants. She sent this crop field in time to save me, so that I could share it with others. The creator wants this crop field to be a gift freely given to all people. She loves all people and wants them to be healed, even if healing looks different for different people.

Tell interrupted her, "but how do you know this?"

Something about Tell's voice made Ru'ah think she was trying to get her to say the truth they all already knew.

"I have spoken to the creator this very day. When Iddo told me the truth of my lineage, the creator came to me to tell me the truth of this crop, the truth of the creator. There it is, there is the truth of the great fire, the truth of this crop, and the truth of the creator. I do not mean to turn anyone away; I want all to come and experience the same miracle I have known. I want all of us humans to know the truth and eat of this crop. Do you believe me?"

Ru'ah looked right at Yri and Beng, the two people who raised her. They were the ones she hoped most believed her. If they continued to stand by her, she could go on. They looked back and her and smiled. She knew then that they were with her to the end.

Ru'ah then chanced a glance of the priests, who were having none of it. Yawen was ablaze with fury, while Iddo looked stunned to her core.

"Enough! Enough of this!" Yawen screamed, pushing away Aratam and Gand with the strength of adrenaline. He sounded like a caged animal ready to attack.

"Warriors you have your orders, destroy the crop, destroy this heathen, destroy everything!"

Again, no one dare move a muscle. Ru'ah, still tied up and sitting in the kindling felt more exposed than ever. The rain had lit up, but the air still hung heavy, as if at any moment the deluge could start. When no one followed Yawen's orders, he turned to his partner, Iddo.

"If you all have chosen to believe this heathen, I have no choice but to call upon the primordial powers of the Great Fire. You have called it a false idol, but I can assure you the Fire is real. The Fire will destroy. I know this, because it runs in my very veins," Yawen said.

He grabbed Iddo, twisting her arm in a most unnatural way. She fell to the ground, screaming in pain. Ru'ah cried out as well. Something deep within her broke as she saw the man who was her father turn on the one who gave her life. Yet she was helpless to watch. Yawen was a madman, lifting up the wick that had once held the flame. With one hand still holding Iddo down, he chanted and danced around, daring the rain to start again.

Ru'ah pleaded for him to stop. She looked over at Tell, pleading the warrior to intervene. But no one moved. Aratam and Gand tried to rush him, but it was as if he was protected by a force field, maybe even one of his own making.

Iddo continued to scream out until Yawen stopped chanting.

"Silence! You are a priest of the Great Fire; you will do what is necessary to serve it!" Yawen said, no sympathy to be found in is voice.

Immediately Iddo stopped screaming. She had remembered her place. Her life had been centered on serving the not only the Great Fire, but Yawen as well. She would do that until the very end.

"Present your throat," Yawen said.

"No!" screamed Ru'ah as her birth mother, kneeling in front of the mad priest, voluntarily exposed her vulnerable neck.

With one more verse of chant, Yawen grabbed the knife out of its sheath with one hand, and a necklace hanging from Iddo's neck with the other. Like lightning he struck the steel knife against the rock pendent. And a flame broke into the air.

Yet, as soon as it appeared it was once again gone. Yawen slashed again. Another flame burned into the wind. Over and over again Yawen slashed, but no flame was strong enough to light the wick again.

Yawen screamed. It was the scream of someone who had felt the sting of ultimate betrayal.

While Yawen screamed, Ru'ah saw Miracle right in front of her. She looked around to see if anyone else saw but realized time had stood still and she was once again alone with the creator.

"Ru'ah, how do you feel?" Miracle asked.

"I'm not sure. I suppose I should feel happy that the priests failed, but I do not," Ru'ah said.

"I am glad to hear that. It is easy to feel satisfied at other's failure, but that is never the right choice," Miracle said. "Look again at the priests called Iddo and Yawen. What do you see?"

Ru'ah looked at them. They were frozen in time and space, but then they started to shift. Ru'ah saw Yawen as a young acolyte, not unlike she had been. He followed the priests around obeying their every command. Not knowing it was his own parents he served.

She saw Iddo being prepared to be united with Yawen and become the Chief Priest. Never having a say in the matter.

She saw Iddo holding her as a baby, longing to raise her as a daughter, but being reminded that she would only ever be the acolyte.

Ru'ah saw Iddo and Yawen for what they really were – products of an environment beyond their control. They were not so different after all. Ru'ah had never had a choice until she made her own choice. Iddo and Yawen made the choice to follow tradition, even if the choice was made unknowingly.

"Ru'ah, how do you feel?" Miracle asked again.

"I feel pity. No, I feel love," said Ru'ah. It was true. For the first time, she looked at Iddo and Yawen not as the Chief Priests of the Great Fire, but as other human beings who were born into the tradition of the Great Fire, who now had the chance to turn away from it.

"What do you want to do?" asked Miracle.

"I want to show them the truth, your truth."

Miracle smiled. It was the most amazing smile Ru'ah had ever seen. She wanted to spend all the time in the world with Miracle. She wanted to hold on to that smile, that moment forever. But she knew it would not be. She had to finish her mission, her true mission that Miracle had given her.

"Now's your chance," said Miracle.

"I'm ready," said Ru'ah.

Time unfroze and Yawen stopped screaming. He fell down beside Iddo, spent from his efforts.

"Tell, untie me please," Ru'ah said.

Tell rushed over to Ru'ah and did as she had been told.

Ru'ah went over to the priest and tried to hold them. They both resisted but only barely. Neither one had much fight left.

"Aratam, Gand, help me get them up. They need to eat of the fruit," Ru'ah said.

In no time the men came over to assist. Satisfied that they were propped up enough to eat, Ru'ah plucked a fresh piece of fruit from the stalk. The air filled with the divine scent of the plant.

Ru'ah said a quiet prayer of thanksgiving to Miracle then ran back to Iddo and Yawen.

Their eyes were glazed over with tears when Ru'ah returned. "Iddo, Yawen, eat of this," she said. Her own mouth longed for the taste of the sweet fruit.

The priests refused. No matter what Ru'ah said or did they would not eat of the fruit.

Yawen went as far as to say, "it is cursed." Ru'ah considered prying their mouths open, but she knew it had to be their choice. She could not force them to eat. And so, she left them. She hoped they would soon change their minds, but she had done all she could do.

Ru'ah stood up to speak with the warriors. They had held position, waiting to see would happen next. Even Tell looked like she did not know what to do.

"Friends, the great fire was a tool given to us by our creator. It is not gone, but it also has no more power over us. We have the power within us, all of us. And just like the great fire, this crop has been given to us as a way of healing. Friends, come and eat of this fruit," Ru'ah said.

Tell was the first to move. She went to the crop field and plucked a piece right off the closest stalk. Again the air filled with the most wonderful scent. She took a deep breath before nibbling at the fruit. Soon she had eaten the whole piece. "I feel completely recovered from battle. Every ache and pain from the march through the desert and the defense of the priests is gone. I haven't felt like this is years."

That was enough to convince the rest of the warriors to take and eat. Soon all were healed of the battle scars, and the deep hurt of seeing the great fire for what it really was. No one said it, but they all could feel the truth overwhelm them. They too had been products of the oppressive society formed in the name of the great fire. They all knew they would never go back to that.

Once everyone had their fill, Ru'ah tried one more time to offer Iddo and Yawen the fruit. They had recovered enough that she wanted to talk with them.

"Iddo and Yawen," Ru'ah said as she slowly approached them. "May I sit with you?"

Yawen would not look at her, but Iddo nodded.

Ru'ah sat down and felt the tension grow. She didn't know what to say, so she let the tension build.

"I suppose you are happy at the way things turned out," Iddo said, her words dripping with venom.

"Happy? No. I am glad everyone has seen the truth. But what would make me happy is if you would taste of the fruit and feel its healing power," said Ru'ah.

She showed the fruit to Iddo. She thought she might have convinced her to try it, but Iddo once again refused.

"We are Chief Priests of the Great Fire, we will not bow down to this false idol," Iddo said.

"I hope one day you will realize that the fire, the fruit, they are all but gifts. I hope you will stay here a while and see the good the crop does for all people," Ru'ah said.

That must have been the last straw for Yawen. He rose to his full height. "The crop is false, you are a heathen. The Great Fire might have abandoned us for now, but we will never turn away from our priesthood," he said. He once again grabbed Iddo's arm and pulled her up. "We will take our leave now."

"Where will you go? Back to Negev? I will go with you if you would have me," Ru'ah said in sincerity.

"We will not have you," said Yawen. "And now that the warriors have turned on us, we are not safe in Negev."

"We will not go back to Negev," said Iddo. "We will go to where all Chief Priests go when their time is done. We will go continue to serve the Great Fire until the end of our days."

"Iddo, let us go now," Yawen said, tugging at her arm. Ru'ah wanted to say something more to make them stay but couldn't think of anything.

The priests were just about out of ear shot when Ru'ah realized that it was she wanted to say. She ran up to them asking them to stop. Yawen must not have heard her because he kept marching. When Ru'ah caught up to them she reached out to get Yawen's attention.

"Yawen, Iddo – you gave me life, you gave me shelter and you taught me the best you knew how. Before you go, I just wanted to say I love you."

Ru'ah watched as Iddo's eyes filled with unshed tears. She wanted to embrace this woman, to feel her embrace as well. But, when Ru'ah looked over at Yawen, her heart broke. He looked at her with nothing but contempt. She might as well have been a fly that ruined his favorite meal. She was nothing to him, more than nothing, she was the nuisance that would not go away.

With one last curse, Yawen kept walking, dragging Iddo behind him. Ru'ah knew she would never see the Chief Priests of the Great Fire, her parents, again.

Ru'ah watched until they were out of sight, then turned to go back to the crop field. This was her new life now, and she would treasure it.

As Ru'ah walked back, she saw that Tell was in scout mode, organizing and ordering her troops. The pilgrims had come out of hiding and needed reassurance that they were safe. Ru'ah knew more pilgrims would be coming and was grateful to have help from Tell.

"You are a natural at this," Ru'ah said as she walked up to the Wise Scout.

"There is a reason I was assigned this job by the priests," Tell smiled back. Then she said something that amazed Ru'ah. "Ru'ah, I want to thank you for your bravery today. I have felt for a while now that there was something not quite right about the Great Fire, but I never would have had the courage to stand up to the priests myself. Now that I know the truth, I will protect it to the end."

"I do not feel like I was brave. I just knew something had to be done, and I did it," Ru'ah said.

"That is bravery," said Tell.

Ru'ah felt radiant. She had admired Tell for so long, and now it was Tell who admired her.

But Tell interrupted her glow. "But, now what? We know the truth, but there are so many others who don't. The priests have so much power; they could easily overcome us."

"I do not think we have to worry about the priests anymore. They have left and will not be returning," said Ru'ah. "If you will help me, I want to start by spreading the truth to all who are here now."

"Yes, I will help you. I will help spread the truth," said Tell. "But, I think it be best if we all rested. The stars are bright in the sky, and we are all weary. Let us feast together, and tomorrow we will start this new mission."

Together, Ru'ah and Tell spend the next few hours making sure the pilgrims felt safe and comfortable. There was still plenty of crop to go around and plenty of room to sleep through the night safely. Ru'ah's heart was full that so many people already knew the truth of the crop. She would not have to walk alone anymore.

Soon, Tell felt like the job was done for the night and sent Ru'ah back to her hut for a good rest. When Ru'ah made it back to her hut, she saw there was already a crowd in it. Yri, Beng, Gand and Aratam had made themselves at home. That made Ru'ah truly happy. Her parents might have cursed her and abandoned her, but her true family was still right here.

"There you are!" Yri said as Ru'ah entered in.

"I'm afraid we lost track of each other in the aftermath," said Beng. "We have been waiting for you here for hours. Is all well?"

Ru'ah sighed and shared with them what happened with the priests. She assured them they were gone and would never come back.

"That means Negev is without protection," Gand said.

Ru'ah nodded in agreement. She knew that to be true but did not know what to do about it right then.

"Tomorrow I will return as its defender," Gand said. Ru'ah realized that as much as she considered the crop field her new home, Gand still felt connected to Negev. Of course, he would want to protect it. In turn, she wanted to stand with Gand as he had stood with her.

"Tomorrow I will tell the pilgrims the truth of the crop of miracles, and then I will go with you back to Negev," Ru'ah said.

"No," Yri interrupted. "We will all go with you."

That seemed to settle the conversation. They would all travel together and spread this good news of the crop.

The hut filled with a silent contentment as Ru'ah just enjoyed the company of the people she loved the most until her stomach reminded her that she had not eaten all day. "I suppose I better collect some more fruit," she said after noticing her reserve had been emptied.
"Ah, there's no need for that," Beng said. "I have the solution to your problem."

Beng revealed that he had been busy with the crop. "This is a delicious fruit on it's own, but I wanted to see how it would taste as an ingredient."

Ru'ah laughed when she saw the array that Beng had prepared. Even with the limited resources of the desert Beng was able to find different ways to prepare this fruit. They all looked equally as wonderful. Beng had always had a way with food, so it was no surprise he used his talents even out here.

"But if the fruit is cooked, does it lose its powers?" Ru'ah asked.

"That's the thing, the more we handled it the more powerful and flavorful it became – almost to the point it was too much," said Beng.

"It also makes a good salve," Yri chimed in. We all had deep cuts from where the scouts had us tied up. I found that simply rubbing the fruit on my skin healed it."

This crop really was a miracle. Nothing seemed to damage it, and it could work its wonders in so many different ways. Ru'ah couldn't wait to share this new information with the pilgrims. But for now, she needed sleep and she needed it badly. Even with the healing powers of the fruit, she felt her body yearning for rest.

She was grateful when Aratam noticed her exhaustion.

"I think we've all had enough excitement for one day," he said to the group. "Let us rest up, for another day is coming."

Ru'ah said good night to her friends, curled up in her sleeping spot and slept a long and dreamless sleep.

The next day Ru'ah awoke late in the morning. Everyone else had already left the hut. She quickly grabbed a bite of fruit Beng had prepared and left to find the others.

She loved the way the new day felt. It was warm and the breeze lifted up the sweet smell of the crop. Knowing that the truth would soon be told filled Ru'ah with excitement like never before. She was ready for this new day.

Ru'ah found her friends conversing with Tell. Apparently, the Wise Scout had informed them of the plan to tell the truth of the crop of the pilgrims. And they had informed her of their plan to return to the Negev afterwards. The only thing left was for Ru'ah to talk to the pilgrims. Tell went to give orders to the scouts to gather the pilgrims, including the ones who had just arrived.

"What do you need from us?" Yri asked.

"Just that remain with me, no matter what," Ru'ah said.

"No matter what," Gand and Aratam said together. She was so pleased that these two men had become such good friends in such as short amount of time.

"They are all here. It is time," said Tell.

"Pilgrims of the Kingdom of Enst, you have come here because this crop healed the family that rules over you. You came to pay homage and to experience the healing power of the crop for yourselves. But now I must tell you that the crop is so much more than you know," Ru'ah said.

Murmurs arose from all corners of the crowd, but Ru'ah continued strong.

"Long ago there was nothing but a creator. That creator made all things, including the great fire and all of humanity …"

Ru'ah went on to tell the crowd about the creator, about the desire to heal the people with this crop and show them the great fire was nothing but a tool for them all to use. She told them about a new society, one that did not have rules or priests or slaves, but a society where all lived and worked together as equals. She told them her truth, the truth she knew deep within her soul. Then she stopped talking to see how the crow responded.

At first there was no reaction. Ru'ah thought back to all those days ago when the pilgrims first showed up. No one wanted to speak for the crowd then as well. She hoped someone would say something soon.

Her wish was granted when an older man piped up. "Why should we believe you?" he said.

This was the question Ru'ah knew was coming, but she did not have a good answer for it.

"I cannot make you believe. All I can say is that I know it's true. If you trust this crop, I ask that you trust my truth as well."

Again, murmuring came from the crowd. No one else said anything but the tension rose.

"The King will not allow such a society," another voice came from the crowd.

This time it was Aratam who spoke before Ru'ah could. "The King knows the truth of the crop. If enough of us profess this truth, he will have no choice but to listen to us. If we stick together, we can create the society that we want."

Ru'ah wanted to say more, say something that would convince this crowd, but she knew within her that the crowd would just need time. The more of the crop they ate, the more they would know the truth.

"Pilgrims, all I ask is that you look within yourself. See what the crop has done for you and your family. Then you will know what we have said it true," Ru'ah said. She looked back at her friends to tell them they were done here; it was time to move on.

The crowd dispersed once again into the field. Newcomers made their way to eat it for the first time. Some packed up to return to Enst, but most stayed in their new homes.

Ru'ah gathered again with Yri, Beng, Gand, Aratam, and Tell. "It is time for us to move on. One day we will come back, but for now we must continue spreading this truth."

"Ru'ah, with your permission I ask to stay here," Tell said. "My scouts and I can greet the new pilgrims and tell them about the crop. I can help spread this truth from here."

Ru'ah embraced Tell. "You do not need my permission. If this is what your mission is, you must do it. I will miss you, but I can think of no one better to stay here and take care of the crop field."

With that, it was time to return to the temple city of Negev.

Chapter Ten

Ru'ah looked back at the crop field one more time as she set out for the return journey. She longed to stay, but knew she had to go. She assured herself that Tell and the scouts would take care of things, but it was still hard to let go.

Before Ru'ah, Yri, Beng, Gand, and Aratam had been able to leave, a guard from the King of Enst found them. He had been present for Ru'ah speech.

"Greetings from the King of Enst," the guard said. "I have been sent here with a message for Aratam, servant of the King, and Ru'ah, keeper of the Crop Field."

Aratam stepped forward to speak to the guard with Ru'ah. "Greetings guard, what is your message?" Ru'ah said.

"As the pilgrims have come back to report on the healing powers of the crop, the king yearns for more of it as well. He has already eaten through the gift you left him with. The king demands that you both return as soon as possible. Aratam, your time has already expired. Ru'ah, the king would like to speak with you further about the crop and the great fire," said the guard.

Ru'ah looked at Aratam. She knew he was thinking the same thing she was - they would not be returning to Enst yet. The guard must have caught their silent exchange because he cleared his throat and said, "Aratam, your king has given you your orders."

"Friend, you heard the truth straight from Ru'ah's mouth. You know I now have no king. I am no longer a slave. I am free and will always be free," Aratam said.

"You may believe what you will, but I will not sacrifice my life failing my king. You will return as has been ordered," said the guard.

Ru'ah thought back to the conversation she and Aratam had while they were in Enst. This is what he had feared. Freedom came with a steep price. The king would need convincing of this new society. Until then they were in danger of retaliation. If the king wanted to, he could bring a force to the crop field and destroy the people. Ru'ah shuttered at how close the priests had been to doing that if the scouts hadn't listened to her. Would they be so fortunate again? Would Miracle continue to intervene for them?

These were questions she could not leave to chance. As much as she wanted Aratam to go with her, maybe the best thing would be for him to go back to Enst for now and she would come as soon as she could.

She was about to suggest that when Aratam spoke up first. "Friend, I have no desire to put you in harm's way on my behalf. You are as free as I am. My freedom does not come before yours. We must all work together for our freedom."

The guard did not look convinced by this, but Aratam continued, "I will send with you as much fruit as you can carry as a gift to the king. I will also send an assurance that Ru'ah and I will come to Enst by the end of the month. This is on my honor."

That must have been the exact right thing to say because the guard agreed. "I will require extra hands to take as much fruit as needed to satisfy the prince."

"I will gather that for you now before we leave," Aratam said. "Ru'ah, will you help me?"

Ru'ah nodded and followed Aratam back to the hut. Together they worked quicky to weave baskets from the discarded husks and fill them with as much fruit as possible while Yri, Beng, and Gand prepared for the journey back to Negev.

Once they were well into their work Ru'ah dared ask her question. "Why did the guard change his mind and allow you to stay behind?"

"Honor," Aratam said. "In Enst, we believe honor is the greatest thing one can give. We live with honor, we serve with honor, we die with honor. If the guard tells the king I have said I will return on my honor, he will be assured I will return."

"But won't the king still be upset with that guard for not bringing you back?" Ru'ah asked.

"Only if I do not return when I say I will. Until then he will honor the guard," Aratam said.

Ru'ah shook her head. She had learned so much about the world in such as short amount of time, but there was still so much to learn. At least she wouldn't have to learn it all on her own.

Once they were satisfied with the amount of fruit gathered for the king, and have given it to the guard, they met up with Yri, Beng, and Gand.

"Ready for the journey home?" Gand asked as they started walking.

Home. Ru'ah could no longer think of Negev as her home. She breathed deeply the scent of the crop field and ate one last bite of fruit for the strength she would need. She did not know how long she would be away or when she would see her field again.

"One day I'll be back," she whispered to herself. Then she sat off back into the desert, but this time not alone.

The journey back was uneventful. Ru'ah enjoyed sleeping under the stars. Each night she tried to count them, but she fell asleep before she even got close to the end. She also loved spending time with Yri, Beng, and Gand. It felt like a weight was lifted from them now that the priests weren't looming. They could talk freely. Yri and Beng told her stories of her childhood that she barely remembered. They also told stories from before she was born. Those were the ones that interested her the most.

"When it was announced Yri was pregnant the whole city stopped. Yawen planned a celebration the likes of which had not been seen. The only one that rivaled it was your coming of age party. Yawen wanted to show off that he had produced an heir. The Great Fire would soon have a new acolyte and then a new priest," Yri said.

Ru'ah thought about what Yawen and Iddo must have felt. Had they loved her then, or had she always been a means to an end? She would never know.

When they had run out of stories of Negev, Aratam shared storied of Enst. He was so animated when he told stories, he rivaled Beng. He told stories of the prince who was now the king. And he shared storied of his own family.

"I think my parents would be proud of what I've done with you and the crop field. And I think they would believe the truth," he said.

"I think so too," Ru'ah said and gave him a hug. She thanked Miracle once again for this person who came into her life seemingly out of nowhere.

On and on the group walked until Negev came into the horizon. The sight took Ru'ah's breath away. They were so close, but she had to ask them to stop.

"I'm not sure I'm ready to return," she said.

She didn't realize the pain she was still carrying from her past. Her whole life in Negev was serving the priests and the great fire. She knew they were no longer there waiting for her, but the pain was still very much present. She sat down in the desert looking at the skyline of the temple city.

She felt someone standing right by her and looked over to see Yri. "I can't imagine what you are feeling right now. We were slaves in the city too, but not like you. We were not enslaved by our own parents. Take the time you need; we will wait with you."

Ru'ah was beyond grateful. She could always count on Yri to put her needs first. Yri, the mother she had always had. She thought of all the times she spent with her, working on fabrics, eating food, walking throughout town. It occurred to Ru'ah that without the temple city she would never have known Yri or Beng or Gand. They had been her family even when she hadn't known it.

She decided then and there that from now on she would think of them when she thought of the temple city, and not of the priests or the great fire. Once that was decided she took a deep breath, reached inside her bag and pulled out a piece of fruit she had brought with her. She ate a good piece and immediately felt better. She could go on; she could face what was waiting for her.

The last leg of the journey was the most ominous. Usually there were scouts posted along the walls of the city, but there was no one when they arrived. Ru'ah knew that some of them had gone to the crop field with the priests and Tell, but surely some of them would have remained behind. Even Gand, a scout himself, looked worried. Ru'ah prayed there was no foul play involved.

Together Ru'ah, Beng, Gand, and Aratam walked through the city gates, and still not a soul was to be seen. The market was empty, and the houses looked boarded up. Had everyone left?

"I would like to check on our house if that is ok with everyone," Yri said.

Ru'ah nodded and followed them through the town. It was so quiet that Ru'ah could hear her heart pounding. They rounded and corner and saw the house they all knew and loved. It looked intact. Beng went inside to see what that looked like while the rest stayed outside. Soon enough he came back out.

"It's the strangest thing, everything looks just as it did when we left," he said.

"So; nothing was gone? Were there any signs of the children?" Yri asked.

"I thought I heard giggling, but I couldn't find the source. Maybe it was just wishful thinking," Beng said.

"There has to be some explanation," Gand said. "The whole city couldn't have just disappeared. Maybe our answer lies there," he said pointing to the temple.

Ru'ah knew they would have to end up there eventually, might as well go there now when she felt strong.

They continued their march to the temple, and still did not see a single person.

Ru'ah looked up the stairs she had walked up so many times before. It was time she walked up them again, she hoped for the last time. She looked at her right and left, surrounded by the very people she would need to do this, took a deep breath, then took the first step.

She climbed up and up without saying a word. She let the feelings of the past wash over her, knowing those feelings would stay in the past. This temple had no power over her. She was free, she was in control. Still, she worried what had happened to the others. Had the priests done something to them before they left? Surely, they would not have been so cruel.

Finally, Ru'ah and the rest reach the top of the stairs. She looked back at the silhouette of the city. It was truly beautiful. She could understand why this spot had been chosen as the spot to worship the great fire.

She looked forward at the doors of the temple. The temple no-one but the priests and the acolyte had been allowed in. How many lonely nights had she spent in that temple? Never again.

Together with Gand and Aratam she heaved the doors open, not knowing what to expect. Hoping for the best but preparing for the worst. What she saw was truly the last thing she expected.

There in the Realm of the temple of the Great Fire was the rest of the community of Negev.

"Ru'ah is that you?" a voice said out of the crowd.

"Yes, I am here with Yri, Beng, and Gand," she replied.

"Where are the priests? Have they not brought you?" the voice asked.

"The priests are no longer rulers of the Negev," she said.

"Then you have taken over as Chief Priests," said the voice. "Citizens of Negev, we must come before the chief priest of the Great Fire and beg forgiveness. In our fear we huddled in this temple. But we all knew what the consequence of our action would be."

Ru'ah looked on in amazement as all the people of Negev kneeled before her. At first, she could not make out their chant, but she soon realized they were simply asking for forgiveness. No one was allowed to enter the temple expect the priests and acolyte on pain of death. These people were begging for their lives, and the lives of their children.

"People of Negev, I assure you, you are not in need of my forgiveness. You have done nothing wrong," Ru'ah said above the chants.

"We have! When we entered into the temple, we took our lives into our own hands," said the voice.

"Tell me then, why did you enter?" asked Ru'ah.

"It was out of fear. When the priests left, they took with them most of the scouts. We were left defenseless. Pilgrims have been so rare these days that our resources have been running dry. We did not know how long we could survive on our own. Then, a few nights ago, a wind came from the west. The wind as so strong it knocked our doors open and blew anything untied away. When it died down, we made the decision to stick together in the temple. We wanted each of us to be safe. And so here we have been ever since then, not knowing what was to come next."

A few nights ago? Ru'ah thought back and realized that wind must have happened the same time the fire had been extinguished by the rain drop. She was so moved with compassion that she decided right then and there to tell the citizens of Negev what happened to the priests and the truth of the great fire and crop field.

It took so long for Ru'ah to get through the story with so many interruptions and questions. Not being in the crop field made it difficult for Ru'ah to fully explain. It was not until she brought the fruit out and showed it to them, that people would even listen.

"I offer this fruit of the crop to you all. Eat it for yourselves and see that it is good," she said to the hesitant crowd.

Slowly the fruit went around the temple. Each person had to hold it and smell it before they would eat it. But, no matter how it was handled, it still filled the whole room with its sweet perfume. Once people began to eat of it, Ru'ah could tell it worked just as well as it had in the field. Perhaps she would be able to convince them of the truth after all.

"This crop is wonderful, for sure," said another voice from the crowd. "But what shall we do without the priests? Who will lead us?"

"That is the beauty of this new truth. We are all free to live together as one. No one will be in charge because we will all work together," Ru'ah said.

Like the pilgrims in the field, this crowd was not convinced of that reality. No one had known freedom yet. No one knew what freedom was really. How did freedom work? How were they to survive if it wasn't in service to someone who would provide for them?

Ru'ah knew it would again take time for the people to learn this way of life. It was not something she could convince them of, it was something they had to accept for themselves. Of course, taking them all to the field would be the best way to show them, but she knew how fearful they would be of leaving Negev, at least for now.

The day had come to its close and Ru'ah felt exhausted.

"Friends, I offer this to you – let us leave the temple and return to our homes for the night. Tomorrow we can continue this new journey together," Ru'ah said.

Ru'ah watched the people get up to leave. The children Beng had been responsible for came running up to him, surrounding him with hugs.

"We missed you!"

"Why were you gone so long?"

"Will you tell us a story?"

Beng, as patient as ever, gave them all the attention they wanted. "I will tell you a story if it is ok with your parents. But they might want to take you home tonight," he said.

Ru'ah's heart swelled, but she left Beng to fend for himself. She knew he could handle it. She wanted to find Aratam, to make sure he was safe. She noticed some had looked at him with curiosity and fear. He was not one of them.

She found him surrounded by a mob who were demanding to know who he was and why he was there. She moved to intervene. "Friends, I ask you trust this man. He has come along with me throughout my journey. He has aided me many times. Trust him like I do."

Immediately the mob bowed down. They still treated her like she was the new Chief Priest. Ru'ah realized that in order for these people to form a new society, she could not be part of it. As long as she was there, they would see her as the inherent leader. She knew she could not let that happen.

She and Aratam walked arm in arm back to Yri and Beng's home. As they walked, Ru'ah saw shadowy figures standing in the ally way between two houses. There were harsh whispers. Two people were having a heated discussion. Ru'ah pulled Aratam along to give these mystery people privacy, until she heard clearly one of the voices.

"You're right, it is time," said Gand.

Ru'ah looked over at Aratam. They must have had the same thought – Gand was up to something with someone. Not wanting to be caught listening in on a conversation that was not meant for them, they rushed into the house. Yri was already there getting ready for the rest of the evening. She had been preparing some fruit, Ru'ah could smell in the air. She didn't realize how hungry she had been.

"I hope Beng and Gand show up soon," Yri said.

Ru'ah looked over at Aratam. Should they tell Yri what they overheard? Aratam shook his head ever so slightly. Ru'ah thought he must be standing up for his friend. They must trust Gand, and the easiest way to lose his trust is to rat him out to his mother. They both kept quiet.

Soon Beng came through the door. "It took a great effort, but I finally fought the children off," he laughed. "Oh, how I missed them all!"

"What story did you tell them?" Ru'ah asked?

"Why I told them a tale of the brave Ru'ah, who, with her wit and heart saved herself and her family," Beng winked.

Ru'ah laughed. Beng certainly had a way of twisting a tale. But she hoped the children knew what they had all done to save them from further oppression.

Beng was helping Yri set the table for the evening meal when Gand finally came through the doors.

But he was not alone. Behind him was the bread maker of Negev – Caff.

Ru'ah was not expecting that. She knew Gand and Caff were good friends, but she expected Caff to be with his own family, not with them. Nonetheless, she was pleased to share the meal with Caff as well. It had been a long time since she had seen him.

But dinner would have to wait. "There is something I have to say," Gand said.

Yri, Beng, Ru'ah and Aratam waited in anticipation for Gand to continue.

"I came of age a few years ago and ever since then you all have been encouraging me to find a partner to unite with," he said to Yri and Beng. "But I have been hesitant. I liked being on my own. Some of the scouts, like Tell, have remained single, so I thought I could too.

I did try to think about who might be a good partner. And I have to admit after her coming of age I looked at Ru'ah differently. I tried to convince myself that she would be the right partner for me. She is stunning in so many ways, it is hard to deny." At that he winked at Ru'ah.

"But the truth is, once Ru'ah left into the desert, I realized I would only ever see her as my sister, my friend." Ru'ah was relieved to hear that.

"The truth is, I have not settled down because I was hiding from my true feelings," Gand said as he turned to Caff. "Caff and I have known each other for so many years. Even though he is older than I am, I feel like we have a connection like no other. He would bring the scouts fresh bread every morning and we would talk and talk. I have shared things with Caff that I have never shared with anyone else. But I could not bring myself to admit my feelings. He confessed his for me some time ago, but I resisted. It wasn't until I thought the priests would kill us all that I realized how much I loved Caff. His was the only face I saw as I thought about what I would miss in my life. I longed to return to Negev just to be with him.

When we saw each other tonight I think we both knew the truth. We love each other now and forever. We want to be together now and forever," Gand finished up his speech.

Ru'ah stifled a laugh. She remembered watching Gand and Caff dancing at her coming of age party and thought there was something different about the way Gand held Caff. She was so pleased for her friend. But not nearly as pleased as Yri.

The mother rushed to her child and hugged him tighter than ever before. "I knew this day would come!" she shouted. She ran back to Beng and hugged him as well. "He found his partner!"

Caff stepped up. "I am so pleased to see how happy you all are. I love your son very much and promise to take care of him."

"No," said Gand, "we will take care of each other."

The family danced around in utter joy. Ru'ah looked over at Aratam who was crying tears of joy as well. His friend had found love and happiness. That made him happy as well.

After the celebration the family, including Caff, sat down to eat. Ru'ah now felt like she could ask the question she wanted to ask every citizen of the temple city.

"Caff, do you believe the truth we shared today?"

Caff did not say anything at first. She could feel Gand shoot her a look that told her to tread lightly.

But Caff soon broke the silence. "When I ate the fruit, I felt safe for the first time probably in my life. I want to believe that you say, because it is so appealing, but I must admit I have my questions."

"What are your questions?" Ru'ah asked.

"First, why did the crop not show up sooner? Why did this Miracle you spoke of not intervene before now?"

Ru'ah considered his question and thought back to her time with Miracle. "I do not have an answer for you," Ru'ah finally admitted. "But I do know that Miracle loves all of us deeply and wants the best for us. Perhaps she wanted us to find the truth for ourselves, but realized we needed a little help."

"Perhaps," said Caff. "I would very much like to speak with Miracle myself."

A sense of agreement filled the room. Ru'ah had no idea how to make that happen. As far as she knew, Miracle had only spoken directly to her.

"Perhaps you should try calling for her," Ru'ah finally said.

Caff laughed. "Perhaps I will, but now I think we should all rest. It has been a long day."

Ru'ah was grateful for him answer. She didn't know how many more questions like that she would have to answer, but she knew they were coming. If not from him, then form others.

Ru'ah lay down to sleep that night in a house for the first time since she left Enst with Aratam. It had not been all that long ago, but it felt foreign. She missed the wind blowing through the hut, and the smell of the crop right outside. She missed hearing the sounds of the pilgrims rustling around – especially the children who had recently been healed. Even though she was not alone in the house, she felt isolated.

After what seemed like hours of tossing and turning, she decided to take a walk around outside. The fresh air hit her as soon as she left the warm home. She took a deep breath, filling her lungs. It was not the same as the air in the field, but it was enough to give her the comfort she needed.

To her surprise Ru'ah realized she was not alone outside. It would seem like someone else was having trouble sleeping as well.

"Is everything ok, Gand?" Ru'ah asked as she sat down next to her brother.

"Yes … and no," he said. "I've been thinking a lot about what Caff said."

"Yes, so have I. Is that why you can't sleep?" Ru'ah said.

Gand nodded. "He makes a point. I've been thinking about those questions as well. It all made sense in the crop field, but now when I'm away from it, it makes less and less sense. How are we supposed to convince other people, if we can't even answer those basic questions for ourselves?" Gand said.

Ru'ah took another deep breath. "Perhaps we can answer those questions," she said.

"What do you mean?" Gand asked.

"I mean I have spoken with Miracle many times now. I feel like I know her. You were in the crop field and ate the fruit. You know it as well as I do. Since neither one of us can sleep, let's figure out answers to our questions." Ru'ah said.

Gand considered this. "But we don't know the answers for sure. Wouldn't that be lying?"

"I don't know, maybe," said Ru'ah. "Or maybe it's relying on what we know to answer questions that we really can't answer. For instance, we know Miracle created everything and loves us, so there must be a reason she waited to send the crop field. Maybe that reason was her perfect timing."

"But that's not really an answer," said Gand.

"Well, it's the best answer I have," said Ru'ah.

Gand nodded again. "It's certainly better than nothing."

For the rest of the night Ru'ah and Gand sat next to one another asking their questions and coming up with answers. By the time the sun rose they both felt like they could use this new knowledge to help others more fully understand. They felt more prepared to spread this news of the crop and new society. Now it was time to test it out.

Caff founded them sitting together outside the house.

"There you are," he said, sitting down next to Gand.

"We think we have an answer to your question from last night," said Gand.

"Already? Let's hear it!"

"We believe that Miracle sent the crop when she did because knew something we didn't know. So, she sent the crop in her perfect knowledge and perfect timing. We just have to have faith that she did so," Gand said.

"So, your answer is to have faith in her perfect timing?" Caff asked.

"Well, yes. That's really the only thing we can have faith in," Ru'ah said.

"Hmm. Well, I suppose. The problem is, I don't know if I have faith in it." Caff said.

Ru'ah and Gand were crushed. Their sleepless night hasn't paid off after all.

"But," Caff said. "I have faith in you. And if you believe in this, I will trust in what you say."

Gand glowed. "I would never lie to you, and I would never lead you astray," he said to Caff.

Maybe that was the answer to all of these questions, thought Ru'ah. It wasn't about having the right answers, it was about being in trusting relationships with people. Once that trust was built it would be easier to spread this good news. Not everyone had seen Miracle firsthand, or even the crop field firs hand. But everyone in Negev knew Gand, Ru'ah, Yri and Beng. That is where they would start, through the relationships already built.

Throughout the next few days, they tried out this new tactic. They all met with citizens of Negev that they already knew. They spoke to them one on one and built trust. They told their own personal stories of the crop field, and the truth Miracle had share with them.

To their amazement, it seemed to work. More and more people started to believe. Society started to shift. People no longer bowed down to Ru'ah and treated her as the Chief Priests. More and more people were asking deeper questions and eating more of the fruit. More and more people showed interested in taking a pilgrimage to the crop field.

Ru'ah was thrilled. Deep within her she felt Miracle's presence. She hoped Miracle was proud of the work she was doing.

About a week after they had returned to Negev, Aratam found Ru'ah in a rare moment of peace.

"Ru'ah I'm afraid it's time," he said.

"Yes, I know. I'm ready to go but I've been hesitant to leave this place on such shaky ground." Ru'ah said.

"I had a feeling you might be thinking that. Let us speak with Yri, Beng, Gand, and Caff this evening. Then maybe you will feel better about going. We must leave tomorrow though, in order to reach Enst before the end of the month."

"We will, on my honor," said Ru'ah.

Evening meal was a solemn event. Everyone knew what must be done, no one wanted to be the first to say it.

"Aratam and I must leave now," Ru'ah finally said after everyone had eaten their fill.

"What will that mean for Negev?" asked Caff.

"I have an idea," said Gand. "Actually, I've been thinking about it for a while."

They all turned to Gand, anxious to hear his plan.

"Yri, Beng, Caff and I all have the necessary skills to take care of this city. Yri can offer clothing, Beng can offer care, Caff can offer food, and I can offer protection. Ru'ah and Aratam must go, but we can stay. We can continue spreading the truth of the crop while using our skills to take care of Negev. Together we can turn this society into one that works together, instead of one that looks to a master."

They all nodded in agreement. "I am willing to do what I can to take care of the people of Negev, until you can return," said Yri to Ru'ah.

Ru'ah wanted to hug her adopted mother. She wanted to tell her how much she loved her and how she would always love her. But before she could do that, she had to share with them her truth. "I cannot come back," she said.

"Why not?" Beng and Yri shouted.

"As long as I am here, there will be those who look at me to be the new priest. The longer I stay the harder it will be for people to move on. And if I come back there is too great of a risk that I will ruin any progress. I must leave so that Negev can change. But I know that you all can do this work. You all can help change Negev," Ru'ah said as tears rolled down her cheeks.

Yri beat her to the hug. Beng and Gand soon joined in. This make-shift family had meant the world to each other. Ru'ah hoped and prayed that they would all be together again someday, somehow. Maybe even in the crop of Miracles.

The sun rose too early the next morning. By the time Ru'ah had gotten up, Aratam was already anxious to go. He had packed as much fruit as could be spared.

Yri, Beng, Gand, and Caff walked them to the edge of Negev. Ru'ah looked out into the desert. She thought about the last time she had set off from this gate. So much had changed. She had changed. She thought about Tell and the crop field. She thought about the priests, somewhere out there still worshiping the great fire. She looked over at Aratam.

"I'm ready," she said.

He took her hand. They said one last goodbye to their friends and family then set off to spread the word of Miracle to Enst and beyond.

www.ingramcontent.com/pod-product-compliance
Lightning Source LLC
Chambersburg PA
CBHW061308210726
48293CB00003B/1167

* 9 7 8 1 9 5 5 5 8 1 6 2 2 *